Praise for *How to Deal with Difficult Customers*

"Dave has done it again! The application of the 10 key strategies in this book will help every sales professional learn how to deal with the *truly* difficult and how to avoid creating *unnecessary* difficulties. It is written with the same wit, humor, and inspiration that have made Dave's prior books so effective."
—Margaret Callihan, President, Chairman, and CEO of Sun Trust Bank, Southwest Florida

"Dave Anderson knocks another one out of the park with *How to Deal with Difficult Customers!* The problem is real; Dave's solutions make sense; and, as always, he makes you laugh in the process."
—Mike Roscoe, Editor-in-Chief of *Dealer* Magazine

"I could not put this book down. It is a salesperson's bible offering clear and concise how-to advice. If you are in the selling profession and want to sell more, you should read this book . . . twice."
—Warren Lada, Senior Vice President, Saga Communications

"An individual executing the ideals within this book will change their own life and their organization. No one has the gift like Dave Anderson to articulate the importance that character plays in maximizing potential."
—Mike Tomberlin, CEO, The Tomberlin Group

"Throw out all your other sales manuals. Dave Anderson's new book will change the way you look at customers, the way your salespeople look at themselves, and quite frankly, the way you look at the sales process."
—Dan Janal, President, PR LEADS.com

"What are you waiting for? We all have difficult customers. If you are tired of leaving money on the table because you can't handle them, read this book. If your good customers are turning into difficult customers, read this book. If you want to deliver results year-in and year-out, read, re-read, and apply the lessons of this book."

   —Randy Pennington, author, *Results Rule! Build a Culture that Blows the Competition Away!*

"Dave Anderson does it again! Implementing the ideas in this book will add up to higher sales, margins, and profits."

   —Bob Farlow, Market President, AutoNation

 "This is not a book about selling theories; rather, it's a 'how-to' manual on proven sales techniques. Dave Anderson writes with authority because he really has been there . . . and succeeded! It will be required reading for everyone on my sales team!"

   —Charlie Polston, Dealership Profitability Consultant, BG Products, Inc.

How to Deal with Difficult Customers

How to Deal with Difficult Customers

10 Simple Strategies for Selling to the Stubborn, Obnoxious, and Belligerent

Dave Anderson

John Wiley & Sons, Inc.

Published by John Wiley & Sons, Inc., Hoboken, New Jersey.
Published simultaneously in Canada.

For general information on our other products and services or for technical support, please contact our Customer Care Department within the United States at (800) 762-2974, outside the United States at (317) 572-3993 or fax (317) 572-4002.

Wiley also publishes its books in a variety of electronic formats. Some content that appears in print may not be available in electronic books. For more information about Wiley products, visit our website at www.wiley.com.

Library of Congress Cataloging-in-Publication Data

Anderson, Dave, 1961–
        How to deal with difficult customers : 10 simple strategies for selling to the stubborn, obnoxious, and belligerent / Dave Anderson.
            p. cm.
        Includes bibliographical references.
        ISBN-13: 978-0-470-04547-3 (cloth)
        ISBN-10: 0-470-04547-7 (cloth)
        1. Selling. I. Title.
    HF5438.25.A5213 2007
    658.85—dc22

                                                                2006014057

Printed in the United States of America.

10 9 8 7 6 5 4 3 2

This book is dedicated to the many SOBs (stubborn, obnoxious, and belligerent customers) I've had the privilege of selling and teaching others to sell over the years. Thank you for forcing us to get better at what we do. Unfortunately for you, your gig is up. You're not that tough. In fact, from this day forward, we're going to earn even more of your money—and make you like the process in spite of yourself.

Contents

Preface

Since time is money for everyone in sales, I'm not going to waste it rambling on through the preface and introduction explaining why I wrote this book. In short, *How to Deal With Difficult Customers* is written for every salesperson on the planet who wants to start making the sales he or she regularly loses to stubborn, obnoxious, and belligerent customers. I can say this with utmost confidence because, regardless of where you sell, what you sell, or how you sell, if you're in the sales profession for more than a few hours you'll encounter a stubborn, obnoxious, or belligerent (from hereon out referred to affectionately as SOBs) customer and have an opportunity to earn his or her business. This book will teach you to sell them more easily, more quickly, and for higher profits.

What inspired this book? Frustration and disgust. Let me explain. I've sold everything from car wax to insurance to carpet cleaning services to automobiles, and it seems that every sales class I ever attended skirted the real-world issue of how to sell to a jerk. Their rationale was, since the vast majority of customers were respectful, pleasant, and professional, why expend time learning to sell someone you may encounter on only 5–10% of your sales calls? Frankly, I needed that 5–10% of the business

I was missing as a result of being unprepared. Over a lifetime, we're talking about a ton of money, and I got sick and tired of wimpy trainers, authors, and managers who didn't seem to think that this segment of the populace was worth learning how to sell or, if the truth be known, didn't know how to sell them. I knew that someone was selling these people and that it should be me. In addition, I wearied of dreading SOBs. They made my life miserable even when I wasn't dealing with them; just anticipating them drained me! What's worse is that I never knew that my own deficient sales skills turned otherwise nice, normal folks into SOBs! In fact, one of the key premises of this book that every salesperson must grasp is that most SOB customers are made, not born, and they're "made" by sales mistakes that can be prevented by applying the strategies in this book.

Over time, I developed a strategy for both preventing normal prospects from turning into SOBs and for selling to genuine SOBs that built my confidence, increased my sales, and made my income skyrocket. Here's a quick sneak preview of what you can expect to find in each of the book's 10 chapters:

Chapter 1: Understand the Ten Truths About SOBs!

Sales professionals must understand some background on what an SOB is and is not if they expect to develop a successful strategy for selling to them. It's also vital to avoid the sales errors that turn Dr. Jekylls into Mr. Hydes. These 10 points set the stage for fully leveraging the other nine strategies.

Chapter 2: Toughen up; Sharpen up; Grow up & Go up!

You cannot grow your career or income bigger on the outside than you are growing on the inside. To sell more SOBs you've got to become mentally tough and drastically improve your skill level. In other words, you must look in the mirror first.

Chapter 3: Don't Just Be Better, Be Different!

If you're no different than most other products or other sales-people your only closing tool will be to have the cheapest price. This is a lousy strategy for anyone making their living on commission. You'll learn how to become not only better than your competition but successfully differentiate yourself from them as well in order to sell SOBs.

Chapter 4: Take the Fight Out of the Sales Process!

Some SOBs want to fight. Others don't want to fight but expect one anyhow because they've become so accustomed to dealing with amateur salespeople. There are key words, phrases, and actions you must use—and avoid using—if you want to remove the fight from the sales process and create a more profitable, amicable closing scenario.

Chapter 5: How to Face and Finesse the SOB "Quadruple Threat"!

There are four common threats posed by SOBs that we'll acknowledge and strategize on how to overcome. These are real world sales inhibitors that aren't going away so you must arm yourself to deal with them effectively and turn them to your advantage.

Chapter 6: Shovel the Piles While They're Small!

When something goes wrong during the sales process or after the sale is made, you need to deal with it quickly, professionally, and humbly. This retains your current customers and brings in referrals as it preserves your own passion and self-esteem. Even when things get totally out of hand and you are assaulted by the most obnoxious of SOBs, this chapter has tools to help you face them down and win.

Chapter 7: Create a Cult!

A key objective of every sales professional should be to become less dependent on fresh customers over time and, instead, build a following of repeat and referral customers that can make you rich. This won't happen by accident. You need to be disciplined, creative, and consistent. By selling more "old friends" you'll have fewer SOBs to deal with.

Chapter 8: Create Urgency to Buy Today!

Your prospects are doing more research than ever before prior to buying a product or service. This means that by the time you see them they are ready to make a decision and to do so quickly. You must leverage this state and create urgency to buy today rather than buying into the nonsense that "people take longer to purchase today" because it's not true. If you get intimidated by an educated customer and don't create urgency for the SOB to buy today, your competitor will.

Chapter 9: Learn to Read an SOB's Mind!

You're going to be much more successful in selling to SOBs if you can learn how they think and pick up on signals they give you, both verbally and nonverbally, throughout the sales process. This chapter covers three aspects of reading your prospects like a book, regardless of the words they're saying.

Chapter 10: Be Prepared to Walk Away!

If you want the deal too bad you probably won't get it—or you'll get it and won't make much money. One of the greatest paradoxes of selling is that to get more deals you can't want them *that* much. This takes fine technique, a tough mindset, and a poker face. This chapter covers seven powerful closes for selling SOBs and outlines seven steps to take if you lose a sale.

After decades of using these techniques and teaching others to do the same I'm going to share these 10 simple strategies for selling to SOBs with you in the coming chapters, and I'm going to do it with straight talk, real examples, and, when necessary, tough love. Don't expect to find silver bullets or one-size-fits-all sales cures for the challenges SOBs present. Selling to SOBs takes plenty of preparation and hard work, and nothing you can do will prove effective every time. Besides, some customers aren't worth having because they bring a negative value to your business (more about that in Chapter 10). But you will find common sense strategies and disciplines that, once applied and internalized into your selling psyche, will make you a calm, confident, closing machine—even in the face of SOBs who make Donald Trump look like Donald Duck.

Each chapter will conclude with an *SOB Summary* that outlines the key takeaways from each of the 10 chapter topics. Think of these summaries as a type of *Cliff Notes* that focuses your thinking on what matters most. The summaries also will make it easier to review what you learned.

We're also going to have some fun along the way. Selling should be fun and so should writing about it and learning about it. We'll poke fun at prospects, other salespeople, and ourselves. Incidentally, if you're always uptight, overly sensitive, and stuck up, you're going to hate the selling profession if you don't already. Loosen up and open your mind and you just might learn something that will change your life, your lifestyle, and the lives of those you serve in sales.

Most of the true sales pros I've met over the years are down-to-earth, uncomplicated, real people and that is precisely who I'm writing this book for. So if you're the academic type, full of yourself, or prone to spend more time whining about why something won't work than giving it a shot, you should have chosen law as your profession and not sales. Nonetheless, my bet is that there is hope even for you if you'll just take a minute or two to get over yourself and adapt the lessons in this book.

Acknowledgments

I'd like to spend a few lines acknowledging that I won't be spending much time on acknowledgments but would be remiss in failing to acknowledge those worthy of being acknowledged. If you're still with me, let's get on with it: I'd like to thank the hundreds of thousands of purchasers of my previous books, cassettes, and CDs because without you this book would not be possible. After all, a publisher is not going to continue letting an author write works that don't sell. In regards to publishers, I'd like to salute editor Matt Holt and John Wiley & Sons for the collaborative spirit, flexibility, and firm support they've offered in the books I've written with them in the past.

About the Author

Dave Anderson is president of LearnToLead, an international sales and leadership training organization. Dave's last "real job" was to oversee the operations of a $300 million retail sales organization, which he left in 1999 to found LearnToLead. His Web site, www.learntolead.com, has tens of thousands of subscribers in more than 40 countries and provides more than 400 free training articles covering a variety of business topics. Dave gives 150 business presentations annually and has spoken in 10 countries. He authors a leadership column for two national magazines and has been the guest on more than 100 business talk radio shows. His interviews and articles have appeared in hundreds of publications, including *The Wall Street Journal* and *Investors Daily*. Dave has authored four earlier books: *Selling Above the Crowd* (1999), *No-Nonsense Leadership* (2001), *Up Your Business* (2003), and *If You Don't Make Waves You'll Drown* (2005). Dave spent many wonderful years living in Texas, but his love of ideal weather and great beaches brought him to Southern California, where his outspoken conservative ideals ensure that he and his wife Rhonda have plenty of time to enjoy these things alone.

Introduction

What makes someone a stubborn, obnoxious, or belligerent customer? In this book, we shall count the ways. But first, in defense of these customers, I should reiterate my assertion from the preface that most SOB customers are not born, they are made. Sadly, many salespeople have become quite proficient at conversions: transforming normal customers into SOBs. It's a form of reverse-evangelism. As a new salesperson, I was no exception. In fact, in the following paragraphs, I'm going to give you an example of how, early in my career, I learned a lesson about these types of sales conversions. Even though it happened decades ago, I can recall clearly how, in the span of 10 minutes, I transformed a nice, elderly, country couple who really seemed to like me into classic SOBs who not-so-politely asked if they could please work with a salesman other than me.

I had just started my job selling cars for Parnell Chrysler—Plymouth—Jeep—Eagle in Wichita Falls, Texas. While stopping by my wife's office to have lunch with her, I noticed an elderly couple hunched over the hood of their old car in the parking lot fiddling with wires in an attempt to start it up. Both Audrey and James wore sweaty cowboy hats, worn-out jeans, and dirty boots and were as country as fried green tomatoes. My sales antenna

went up, and in just a few moments after going out to introduce myself, they made it clear that they were sick and tired of
their clunker and ready to buy something else. I quickly loaded
them up in my car and drove them to the dealership. Audrey
and James couldn't thank me enough for offering to help out
and were genuinely grateful I had been in the right place at the
right time to help them. They confided that they never bought
new cars because they didn't like the depreciation but would be
interested in looking at a reliable used model. I just knew that I
was in store for an easy sale.

After arriving at the dealership, I walked them over to a
line of used cars and began opening up the doors, popping the
hoods one after the other and telling them what I knew about
each one: miles, equipment, remaining warranty, price, etc. After
about 20 minutes standing in the Texas heat and listening to my
used-car speeches, these kind, old country folks looked oddly at
one another and then James spoke up and asked tersely with his
finger pointed at my chest, "Is there an experienced salesperson
here that we can talk to? We ain't gonna waste time looking at
stuff we don't want." I was crushed at their change of heart toward me. I sure had misjudged these people. They were just a
couple of belligerent old codgers who obviously enjoyed pushing younger people around. Embarrassed and angry, I asked them
to hold on while I went to get Bobby Laird, a veteran salesman
who had been the sole team member to introduce himself after
I had started working at the dealership a few days before.

Bobby came out, introduced himself, invited James and Audrey inside for coffee, made what I thought was far too much
small talk, finally got around to asking what kind of car they
had in mind, took them back out into the Texas stickiness and
in less than 30 minutes sold them a car that was twice the price
of the cars I had shown them. I looked on in shock as these two
"hillbillies" wrote a check for the entire purchase.

I was exposed to some valuable lessons that day, although it would take me much longer to actually learn them: The first one being that many SOBs don't start out that way; it takes an unskilled salesperson to bring them down to that level.

As you learn more about how to sell to difficult people throughout this book, it's important to understand why customers are or become stubborn, obnoxious, and/or belligerent. Once we know the "why" we can learn to sell them with a different "how." Here are seven of the top reasons that I'll introduce here and build on throughout the book:

1. They have low expectations about the salesperson and the sales process. Customers have been treated indifferently and unprofessionally in so many instances and for so long that many of them have a bad attitude toward you and the sales process before you even say your first few words. They expect the worst, and, as a profession, salespeople oftentimes live down to their expectations. My guess is that when you are on the purchasing side of a product or service you experience this yourself far more often than you like. Poor or indifferent treatment you receive when you try to spend your money with someone can turn you into a monster—especially if it happens when you're already having a bad day.

2. They have high expectations from the salesperson and company. Unlike point No. 1 above, many customers have a very high set of expectations when they buy. This is created by corporate marketing and advertising that over promises to prospects, almost ensuring that they are let down when they actually come face-to-face with the reality of dealing with the misrepresented organization. This makes people feel deceived and even cheated, which creates a very unpleasant sales experience indeed.

3. They have less time to waste buying a product or service. While more information is available to consumers today and many will spend additional time researching a product or service before purchasing it, they are less likely to want to then waste extra time trying to buy it as they deal with salespeople who turn the sales process into "amateur hour," much like I did with James and Audrey. In fact, because customers who do more research are more certain of what they want they expect to spend less time having to buy it and can turn ugly when this proves not to be the case.

4. Unskilled salespeople who waste their time. Many customers have no intention of being stubborn, obnoxious, or belligerent but are reduced to these attitudes when confronted with an unskilled salesperson who doesn't know how to build rapport, investigate wants and needs, present or demonstrate a product effectively, address objections, close the sale, or competently and expeditiously complete the paperwork involved. Again *wasted time* will frustrate a customer who, in today's world, is wearing more hats in his or her personal and professional life and is being stretched like Gumby in a dozen directions simultaneously by friends, family, coworkers and his or her own customers.

5. Unknowledgeable salespeople who waste their time. Many salespeople are skilled in selling but lack product knowledge and cannot adequately or correctly answer a prospect's questions. When prospects feel they are dealing with someone who doesn't know what he is talking about or who is trying to bluff his way through serious concerns and questions, they can't help but feel a bit ornery and respond with impatience or even anger.

6. Unmotivated salespeople who turn the sales process into a drag. Some salespeople are both highly skilled and knowledgeable about what they sell but have so little passion or enthusiasm that trying to buy from them is like making a date with the walking dead. The mere proximity of these zombies suck the energy out of a room and out of a sales encounter. This is especially true when a prospect is making a large or emotional purchase. In this case, they'd like to see their excitement shared by the salesperson. When the salesperson doesn't deliver, it slows the customer down and can turn a sure-fire buyer into a stubborn looker who will plunk down his or her dollars into the hands of the next fired-up salesperson they meet—even if the product was not the buyer's first choice or costs a bit more than he or she had in mind.

7. Some people are just plain miserable. Nothing and no one makes them happy. These SOBs are to be pitied. Somewhere in their life they started making some bad choices: to trust no one, to never be happy, to see the problem in every opportunity and the list goes on. These people don't necessarily dislike or hate you personally; they dislike and hate much about life, period! Yet, they still must buy and someone's going to sell them. The best revenge against this brood, this fellowship of the miserable, is to make the sale and take their money.

In *How to Deal with Difficult Customers,* I will discuss strategies for remedying all seven of these situations. You'll see clearly that the first step to selling SOBs is to learn how to stop creating them in the first place. And you'll also pick up some effective tools for selling the true-blue SOB who hates the world, hates what you're selling, and may even hate you—not through any fault of your own but just because he or she is a real SOB.

As a natural result of improving your skills to sell the most difficult customers, you'll find that you'll be improving your ability to successfully sell all types of customers, not just SOBs.

In fact, once you master the art of selling to the stubborn, obnoxious, and belligerent, many of the "normal" customers you have the opportunity to sell each day will become putty in your hands and money in your pocket.

You're not likely to internalize the 10 simple strategies I present with just one casual reading of the book. Take good notes, invest in a highlighter, and underline key passages you can refer to again. You'll also benefit from writing the page numbers where you made highlights on the inside book cover so they're easy to reference over time. In other words, don't just get through this book, get from it! Make it pay over and over again.

Here's a word of caution: There are sample scripts that you can use with SOBs throughout the book. These are my words and need not be your words; they are merely guides. Say what sounds natural to you. It's not important that you sound like me. What's important is that you're the best, most believable you that you can be. Because of limited space and time, I'll use sales examples from various professions with the full belief that you will be able to take the concepts presented and fit them to the products and services you sell. Incidentally, the first three chapters are the most intense. Just as it takes more work to lay the foundation when building a skyscraper, only to see the rest of the building come into being quickly by comparison, so must we spend adequate time building your foundation in Chapters 1 through 3 that will serve as your success platform as you absorb chapters 4 through 10. Well, I've already said more than I intended in these opening pages, so before you feel that I'm wasting your time and turn into an SOB, let's get started.

1

Understand the Ten Truths About SOBs!

Let's Start With Straight Talk

This is an information-packed, high-impact chapter. If you haven't yet gotten the pen or highlighter I recommended earlier, get it now. You're going to need it, and you'll be darned glad you got it. Even the toughest customers need the products and services you offer. Someone will sell them. That someone can be you if you can develop a handful of skills and courageously apply them at the right time. I once had an SOB say right after I had introduced myself, "You remind me of the last guy who sold me a car . . . only you're not buried in my backyard." Not all difficult customers are this obnoxious, but the more you understand about them and how to prevent them in the first place the faster and more profitably you'll sell them. Following are 10 truths about SOBs that will help provide the perspective we'll build on throughout the rest of the book.

The Ten Truths

1. Don't judge a customer as "difficult" too quickly based on the first few minutes of your sales encounter. Prospects often put up a tough front early on as a defense mechanism. This can change quickly once they surmise that you are a professional who cares about them and their needs.

2. Understand the three top concerns of difficult customers. While SOBs have many concerns, the top three can be summed up as: Will you waste my time? Do you know what you're doing (are you a professional)? Can I trust you?

3. When you encounter an SOB and he or she says or does something provocative, respond to the customer; don't react to him or her. In other words, slow the SOB down before things spiral out of control. When a customer says something provocative, abusive, sarcastic, and so on, don't take it personally. More than likely it is the buying process itself; it's the thought of spending money or past unpleasant sales experiences the customer is attacking and not you. Here are three tips to help you pull this off:

> A. To slow down the momentum an offensive customer gains against you, increase the space between stimulus and response. This is a classic technique and Stephen Covey communication tip that works wonders for maintaining composure and regaining control of potentially volatile or awkward situations. Don't be too quick to answer a provocative, offensive, or sarcastic statement. By increas-

ing the space between a customer's comment and your reply you gain stronger control over your emotions, have a moment to think more clearly about your reply, and increase the integrity of your answer by giving it the appearance of being more thoughtful.

B. To slow the customer down, reply with a question rather than with an answer. This will oftentimes reveal the core issue and soften the customer's next reply. Be sure to diagnose carefully before offering reckless solutions or responding haphazardly with a confrontational tone. Sell with questions, not just answers.

C. Go low and slow with your tone and speech. Drop the tone of your voice a notch and speak more deliberately. This technique settles you down, takes control of the conversation, and reassures the customer as well. This is a strategy that also works well when closing "normal" customers.

4. Listen with the intent to understand the customer, not to reply to or one-up the customer. This is another tried and true Covey strategy. Until you give customers "air" and let them express themselves, they will not be open to what you have to say. This is especially true if they are the Type-A personalities with chips on their shoulders. Customers don't buy when they understand; they buy when they feel understood.

Take a look at the following sample script and learn what to do as well as what not to do when responding to an SOB's provocative statement:

CUSTOMER: "The price you're asking is absolutely ridiculous!"

INEFFECTIVE REPLY, normally spoken defensively and

quickly: "I don't set the prices. This is what our product is bringing. But we'll make you a good deal on it."

EFFECTIVE REPLY, spoken slowly and sincerely: "When you say the price is too high, Mr. Prospect, could you tell me too high as compared to what?

(This reply slows down the customer and puts you in control by asking a question. It will also help surface the obstacle more precisely.)

CUSTOMER: "Too high compared to what XXX Competitor was selling theirs for across town."

INEFFECTIVE REPLY: "Well, I guess they know what their product is worth. Their lower price is probably an indication that you're not going to get very good service after the sale."

EFFECTIVE REPLY: "I'd be very surprised if someone would beat us on price if their product was exactly the same as ours. Could we take a minute to review the features to be sure we're comparing apples to apples? Did they by ch ance give you their price in writing with a features list so we can compare?"

This slows the customer down even more and leads to an opportunity to raise doubt about the deal he or she was getting elsewhere and to build value in your product and in your professionalism since you haven't had to disparage your competitor or their product. This professional and thoughtful approach will earn the respect of SOBs and normal folks alike.

5. Never say "no" to an SOB. "No" is a fighting word and can be avoided with some practice and skill. The following script will teach you how to say "no" without saying those exact words by offering a way to meet the customer's demands and putting the ball back in his or her court. We'll use an example I'm quite familiar with: selling a car where the customer wants an unrealistic payment. You can apply this same technique to other products and services as well.

> CUSTOMER: "I can pay you $350 per month and no more."
>
> INEFFECTIVE REPLY: "There's no way we can get to that payment on this product. We'll need to look at something cheaper."
>
> EFFECTIVE REPLY: "Mr. Customer, we can reach your payment of $350 per month as long as you can put $2,500 down, would be willing to lease rather than purchase the product, would agree to payment terms of 72 months," and so on.

You can always use the "takeaway" technique used in the first response as a last resort, but try to sell difficult customers what they want. Even if they can't meet the terms they will appreciate the fact that you showed them a way they could own it if they wanted to.

If you're selling radio advertising, the conversation should sound something like this:

> CUSTOMER: "I don't want to pay $125 per spot. I only want to pay $95 per spot."
>
> INEFFECTIVE REPLY: "Mr. Customer, there are radio stations out there with less market share where I'm sure you can get the $95 per spot, but it's not going to happen on our station."
>
> EFFECTIVE REPLY: "Mr. Customer, the great thing about

our pricing is that you get to vote your own discount based on the quantity of spots you purchase. If you want to pay $95 per spot, you can get that price by switching to this package right here."

You can use this "vote your own discount" technique whenever you're selling a product or service that offers a quantity discount.

6. Let the SOB take a bow. Throughout the sales process, acknowledge your customer's expertise and great negotiating skills. Don't be one of those sissified sales wieners who runs the other way when a prospect looks intimidating because he or she comes to your place of business with a clipboard full of notes and printouts from *Consumer Reports.* Use sales skill and sound psychology: *The best way to knock a chip off someone's shoulder is to let him or her take a bow.* Put your ego aside and tell the SOB, "You've really done your homework. That actually makes my job easier because it's always more pleasant to deal with an educated customer." You can also penetrate an SOB's know-it-all demeanor with this humble, but effective phrase: "I wouldn't be at all surprised if you know more about this product than I do! We're always looking to hire great people if you ever decide to switch careers."

You have to admit that it's hard to be tough on someone who pays you a sincere compliment. Use this law of human nature to your advantage when taking the fight out of an SOB.

7. Choose your battles carefully. Don't get bogged down in trivial battles with a tough customer just to feed your own ego. Remember, you can win the battle and still lose the war when the customer decides not to buy what you're selling. It doesn't make much sense to be right and broke! Remember what author and motivator Jim Rohn said, "Don't major in minor things."

8. Remember, difficult customers want to be followed up with if they don't buy from you the first time around. This one takes discipline because your first inclination after an SOB encounter where you don't sell the prospect may be that of "good riddance!" But here's where you must leave your ego behind once again and turn pro in sales by discipling yourself to call back the customer and make another run at closing the sale.

Tough, hard-to-please customers normally know they are unpleasant to deal with and will respond favorably to a salesperson who calls them back quickly to work for their business if they missed it the first time around. It also shows you aren't intimidated by them and this will place you in a better negotiating position the next time you try to close the sale.

This question often arises: How soon should I call the prospects back if they don't buy from me the first time I visit with them? My answer may make you uncomfortable: the same day or the next morning, depending on what time of the day you had them as your customer. This may sound like a pushy way to sell, but that is only the case if you don't use the proper strategy when calling the customer. After all, the difference between pressure and persistence is technique. Read the following script and ask yourself if you'd be more likely to be offended or impressed if a salesman who was trying to sell you called and said these words.

SALESPERSON: "Mr. Prospect, this is Dave Anderson at Golden Rules Jewelry, and I wanted to call you and thank you for the time you spent with me today. I know that many times after customers leave me questions pop into their minds that they wish they'd asked when I was with them, so I wanted to follow up to see if any questions or concerns arose for you that I could address at this time?"

At this point, the SOB oftentimes gives you his or her real objection for not buying. After all, it's easier to divulge this information when he or she is not standing in front of you. Quite often these customers do have questions they forgot to ask or wished they had clarified when they were dealing with you, and this gives you a chance to answer them and move them closer to the sale. In the event the prospect responds to you with, "No, I don't have any questions. You did a good job; we're just not ready to buy yet," you can counter with:

> SALESPERSON: "Mr. Prospect, I can certainly understand the challenge in trying to find the perfect time to buy. But if there was one thing holding you back from moving forward and getting involved with our product, what is it?"

At this stage you have nothing to lose and have just given the SOB a chance to give you something to work with: a concern or objection, which when handled properly moves you closer to the sale.

I don't know how it works in all businesses, but in the automotive retail business, the closing ratio for a customer you get back in the door the second time goes from around 12% when he or she first walked into the dealership to 66% when he or she comes back.

Incidentally, if this approach fails to move you closer to the sale, you're still not done. Wait until you have new information (an upcoming sale, a change in financing terms, a special incentive that's ready to disappear, new inventory that just arrived, etc.) and then call the customer back to share it with him or her and try to schedule the second appointment.

9. SOBs don't like to be rushed. So you can forget about skipping any of your sales steps! Because SOBs can seem in a hurry, it's often tempting to skip or shortcut part of the sales process: taking time to build rapport, asking enough questions to diagnose their wants and needs, spending enough time during the presentation and demonstration focusing on the aspects of your product that mean the most to them, and so on. Warning: If you get in a hurry to close the deal and start skipping steps to the sale you are committing sales suicide! Just as with normal customers, the more time you spend on the steps leading to the close, the less time you actually have to spend closing the deal with SOBs. But the reverse is also true: The less time you spend on the steps to the sale, the *more time* it takes to close the deal because the prospect isn't sold on you, the product, or your company and isn't adequately motivated to make the purchase.

Following the sales steps means . . . :

A. You must develop the discipline to do the right thing day in and day out. This means you follow the steps whether you feel like it or not—on the good days and the bad days, when you're on a roll, in a rut, or somewhere in between. Developing discipline means you do the *right thing* not the easy thing.

B. You spend enough time uncovering wants and needs so that you match the prospects with the product or service that works best for them. Remember: Diagnose before you prescribe! Your closing efforts are wasted when you try to close the deal on the wrong product or service. Your only closing tool at this stage is to drop your price—not the position you want to be in when trying to close the deal with an SOB. Remember, sell the customer what best fits his or her needs—not what you like or want to sell. It's not about you! It's about the customer!

C. You treat everyone in the buying party with respect and you do not prequalify your customers. Prequalifying means you try and guess who is serious about buying or who can afford your product based on the way they are dressed, what they drive, and the like. In short, prequalifying is for fools! You're not good enough at this profession to guess who can and cannot afford your product or who is a serious buyer—no one is! You'll be wrong far more often than you're right. Prequalifying is a form of arrogance. It's also a form of laziness because you try to find a reason *not* to do your job and spend adequate time with the prospect. To make matters worse, you can transform a nice, normal prospect into an SOB when he or she feels you're prequalifying him or her. Needless to say, if you get in the habit of prequalifying, you'll find yourself with fewer chances to close the deal because you'll never get far enough to make it happen. Treat people like buyers until they prove they aren't. Many of them will pleasantly surprise you.

D. Trigger the SOB's positive emotions. The customer begins to take mental ownership during the presentation and demonstration stage of the sales process. Thus, there is much at stake during the presentation and demonstration steps. Trigger the prospect's positive emotions favorably and you'll soon find yourself with a closing opportunity. Drop the ball here and you'll soon find yourself waiting for another customer.

Tips for compelling presentations and demonstrations:

(1) Don't overwhelm the prospect with too much product knowledge. Talk about the features you discovered during your investigation that are most important to the customer. Remember the 80/20 Rule application for selling: Find the 20% of the features the prospect is hottest about and spend 80% of your time focusing on those things during your presentation. When you talk about the things that interest him or her the most you raise the value of your product, but when you ramble on about things he or she could not care less about you simply raise the price of the product.

I can recall early in my sales career when I attended a 2-day Jeep seminar put on to teach us sales reps everything possible about the Jeep product. It was a great class, and I learned so much I couldn't wait to get back to the dealership and wait on my first Jeep customer. The result? I didn't sell a Jeep for weeks after returning to the dealership! Why? I talked too much. I tried to tell each customer everything I had learned about the Jeep and totally overwhelmed and confused them. Some of you may know everything about your product but are still selling very little of it. Could you be making the same mistake I did? Do us both a favor and learn from my stupidity. Know everything possible about your product or service but present it selectively!

(2) Don't beat around the bush when you begin your presentation: Start with the features that most interest the prospect. Canned, panned presentations are the kiss of death in sales. Customize your presentation to fit the prospect rather than trying to fit the prospect into your presentation.

(3) Involve the prospect with questions throughout your presentation. Without involving your prospect with questions strategically sprinkled throughout your presentation, your presentation turns into a speech and the prospect turns into an escape artist at the first available opportunity. Regardless of what you may think, you cannot make a six-figure income in sales by attempting to bore people into buying!

(4) Test the waters. Trial closes are essential to setting up the final close. They let you determine where you and the prospect are in the sales process. When you ask a trial close, nothing bad happens: You'll either close the deal or flush out an objection that will get you closer to consummating the deal. The most appropriate time to ask a trial close is during or at the conclusion of the presentation or demonstration. Timing is important. You must make certain you've created enough value in the product before asking a trial close. You must earn the right to ask these questions. If you ask before you're at a stage where the value presented is equal to or greater than the price you're asking, you'll irritate and offend normal customers and turn them into SOBs, and you'll turn an SOB into an even meaner, uglier beast.

When you ask a trial close it is essential that you make it sound natural and keep your tone and delivery casual and matter-of-fact. A sudden change in tone, pitch, or delivery will alert and possibly alarm the prospect that danger lies ahead: He or she is going to be asked to actually buy something! The key to asking any closing question is to make it sound like conversation, and the key to making it sound like conversation is to practice, practice, practice! This brings up a key point: If you want to turn pro in sales and begin selling more SOBs, you'll need to develop a practice ethnic. After all, if all you've ever done is run around the block and you endeavor to run a marathon, you'll need to intensify your training regimen. Same goes for sales.

The most effective trial closes offer an alternate choice for the customer to pick from. These questions eliminate the yes-no type questions that often kill sales. Ask an SOB a "yes" or "no" question and you'll hear "no" a lot. SOBs like better choices. They don't like to feel that they're being backed into a corner.

Use trial closes like these depending on where you are in the sales process. Change the words to make them sound like you, but retain the same casual, either-or manner of delivery.

A. "Mr. Prospect, it seems like we've found the perfect car for you and your family. Are you going to want the paperwork in your name or the company name?"

B. "Mr. Prospect, it looks like this package provides all the features you told me were most important to you. Would you prefer we begin the schedule by the end of this week, or would you prefer starting after the holiday?"

If you've followed the other steps leading up to the trial close, this technique will seem like a natural progression in the sales process. However, if you skipped steps, trial closes can seem inappropriate, high pressure, and out of place.

10. The tenth truth about SOBs is that you'll never learn to sell more of them by reading the previous nine truths only once. Review them often and internalize them into your sales psyche and you can become unstoppable. As coach Vince Lombardi said, "The harder you work, the harder it is to surrender."

The level of your practice will determine the level of your play. In other words, if your performance isn't what it should be, take a look at the quality and quantity of your practice disciplines. That's probably where the problem is, which takes us to the next chapter.

SOB Summary for Chapter 1: The Ten Truths About SOBs

Even though it hits our egos below the belt to make this admission, it is nonetheless true: We turn otherwise normal customers into SOBs more often than not with deficient sales skills or a lousy attitude. Yes, there are the dyed-in-the-wool stubborn, obnoxious, belligerent bullies who seem to want to pick a fight (and we'll learn techniques for selling them as well), but most of the sales we miss during our careers will result from self-inflicted damage. Avoid sales sabotage with SOBs by understanding the following 10 truths:

1. Don't label a prospect as an SOB too quickly. Many greet you with a tough and defensive manner until they're sure whether or not they like, trust, and believe you.

2. Understand the three top concerns of SOBs: (a) Will you waste my time? (b) Do you know what you're doing? (c) Can I trust you?

3. Respond, don't react, to the provocative attitudes or words of SOBs. Slow down their assaults with thoughtful questions and a low, slow tone and demeanor.

4. Listen to SOBs with the intent to understand, not the intent to reply or one-up them. They will not try to understand you until they first feel understood.

5. Never say "no" to an SOB. Always give them options to get what they want.

6. Feed the SOB's ego by letting them take a bow.

7. Choose your battles with SOBs carefully. Don't get so bogged down in the trivial that you lose sight of the ultimate.

8. If you don't sell SOBs the first time out, follow up quickly and with purpose.

9. Don't rush SOBs through the sales process by skipping vital sales steps that backfire on you later. The longest distance between meeting the customer and trying to close the deal is a shortcut.

10. Review these nine truths often until they're woven into your sales psyche and daily disciplines. Repetition is the mother of skill.

2

Toughen up; Sharpen up; Grow up & Go up!

Let's Start with Straight Talk

There are parts of this chapter that you may be tempted to take personally. Please don't. Life is too short for pity parties. Besides, I don't know about you, but I'm sick and tired of hearing people whine out excuses about why they're not doing better than they are in sales and in life. In fact, more and more people simply amaze me today. They've become experts at concocting explanations and victim stories to explain away their lack of success. So here's a fair question: How can you expect to sell the most difficult customers on the outside if you're not right on the inside?

Your managers can teach you selling skills and product knowledge. But there are a handful of critical success factors in sales that no one can teach you and that are necessary for you to sharpen up, grow up, and go up in sales. You are responsible for cultivating, developing, and brining these traits to the workplace. Without these attributes your success will be inconsistent and all the training in the world won't be able to make you great at selling. What this means is that the only way you can sell more of the SOBs you see standing outside the window is to toughen up, sharpen up, and straighten up the person looking back at you in the mirror. As promised earlier, Chapters 1 through 3 are the most intensive. This one will hit some of you hard, but it's necessary because you can't get too fancy in any profession until you've mastered the basic blocking and tackling. I hope you're up for it.

Toughen Up & Grow Up!

1. Unteachable #1: Character. Your character is a sum of choices you've made throughout your life that have formed the behaviors and values that determine the way you consistently act. Character reflects your habits of the heart. By the time you enter the workplace your character has long been formed. You can change yourself, but no one can change you in this regard. There are no three-day character clinics you can check yourself into and leave all cleaned up on the inside.

Frankly, the selling profession has suffered enormous damage to its image over the centuries because it has its share of charlatans. If you're one of these people—and you know who you are—go do something else for a living. Your failure to live with integrity affects us all.

Thoughts on Character:

A. It is formed over time and revealed most blatantly during tough times. You are not made in crisis; you are revealed in it.

B. It is never inherited but is developed. And for better or for worse, character always has consequences.

C. Character tests are gauged by more than whether or not someone lies, cheats, or steals. Character also involves the following:

(1) Are you teachable? If you've assumed a "been there, done that" attitude that causes you to hate training meetings, tune out constructive criticism, or stop reading books or listening to CDs in your field, you have developed an intelligence arrogance that becomes a disabling ignorance. If you want to learn how to sell more of the most stubborn, obnoxious, and belligerent customers it's essential that you continue to learn more about selling. "Know it alls" have serious character flaws and here's some humbling news: You're probably not as good as you think you are, so go ahead and get over yourself— everyone else has.

(2) Do you persist in the face of difficulties? If you throw in the towel because things get tough or have left in your life's wake a history of quitting, this indicates character weakness. Somewhere along the line you'll need to make a stand and tough it out. In fact, one of the key reasons people fail in sales is they don't stick with it long enough to develop the skills, habits, and attitudes that would make them successful. Successfully selling to SOBs means you'll have to toughen up and become more resilient with customers than you have been in the past.

"Success in life is determined by your ability to go from failure to failure without loss of enthusiasm." —Winston Churchill

---

(3) Do you have a strong work ethic? If you're lazy, you'll never sell many SOBs because you won't have the discipline required to be successful with this group of prospects. You might luck into a charitable SOB once in a career who just won the lottery, takes pity on your pathetic efforts, and looks at buying from you as making a donation, but that's about it. Seriously, if you only work hard when someone is watching you, this indicates character weakness. It also makes you a very undesirable employee. In fact, if you've developed the habit of doing just enough to get by, just enough to get paid, and just enough not to get fired, you've made yourself quite expendable. Your character is also revealed when you decide to continue to push yourself—or not—even while you're doing well, because it shows whether or not you can survive success and avoid pitfalls of arrogance and selfishness.

(4) Do you keep promises and meet deadlines? Failing to keep your word is a character flaw, and it's also one of the fastest ways to turn your teammates against you and to convert a normal customer into an SOB. Do what you say you'll do even when it's tough. If your word isn't worth much, then you're not worth much to your employer, teammates, or customers—and anyone else you know in life who has to listen to you for that matter. Do what you say you'll do, by when you say you'll do it, and how you say you'll do it.

(5) Do you admit mistakes? Failing to admit mistakes should be considered a sin of omission and, thus, is a character ding. Trying to cover up mistakes or lie your way out of them when selling to an SOB ensures you skip right down the yellow brick road and smack into a wall of irrelevance. If you screwed up, admit it. If you were wrong, say so. It liberates your own conscience and helps you connect with others at the same time.

(6) Do you accept responsibility for your actions? Playing the blame game is one of the most repugnant of all character flaws. It means you live in denial. It indicates you may have grown old but haven't grown up. It also means you'll ostracize yourself from productive, responsible people and eliminate yourself from any chance of promotion to a higher station at work and, most probably, in life. Stop blaming the world for why you can't sell the toughest customers. The truth is you can sell them, but you've just got to work a little harder on yourself first. Take this advice from Dr. Phil to heart: "By convincing yourself that you are a victim you are guaranteed to have no progress. . . . If you truly want change, and you truly acknowledge that you create your own experience, then you must analyze what you've done or haven't done to create the undesirable results. Stop saying, 'Why are they doing this to me' and start saying, 'Why am I doing this to myself? What thoughts, behaviors, and choices can I change to get a different result?'"

"I can help take someone from failure to success but I can't take them from excuses to success because if you're making excuses you haven't yet realized where the real problem lies." —John Maxwell

---

There are certainly other areas we could add as character-weakness indicators, but this is a good start. I know I was hard on you in some of the six areas offered, but for good reason: You can control these areas; you can work on them and improve them with greater awareness, reflection, and discipline. No one can do it for you. Character is a do-it-yourself project. Of course it helps if you have some type of spiritual life that offers clear guidance on building a worthy character.

Strengthening or Rebuilding Character:

A. Since character is formed by your choices it can only be strengthened or rebuilt through making better choices.

B. Focusing on doing the right thing even when it is the tough thing is a true test of character.

C. Develop your own spiritual life. Most religious encourage doing the right things for the right reasons. Knowing what to do normally isn't the issue: Finding the faith and resolve to do it is where a stronger spiritual connection can help.

You cannot build a great sales career or an outstanding life by making the habit of doing what is cheap, easy, popular, or convenient. You get to the top by doing what is right. And what's right is often difficult and creates discomfort and pain. But if you don't work through the discomfort and pain of change and growth, you won't advance. You won't even stay the same. Eventually, you'll decline.

2. **Unteachable #2: Drive.** Another person can stroke the embers in an attempt to fire you up but getting the fire going in the first place is up to you. No one can make you driven. No one can make you ambitious. No one can make you "want it." Without drive, there is little hope for you to ever become excellent at anything.

Attendees to my seminars will sometimes come up and confide, "I just don't have any drive. How do I get going?" I startle them by replying—only somewhat tongue-in-cheek—that there is absolutely nothing I can do for them and to please get away from me before I catch what they have. Sales professionals must realize that their manager can't put in what was left out; they can only draw out what was left in. In other words, you have got to give the universe something to work with!

Thoughts on Drive:

A. Oftentimes people who don't feel driven do indeed have drive within them. It just takes the right event, circumstance, or purpose to uncover it.

B. Someone having drive often has it satisfied once he or she reaches a certain level of success. Before the person reaches that point it is imperative that he or she enlarges his or her goals or purpose in order to keep the fire burning.

C. Many times getting better at what you do will increase your drive and motivation since you will be anxious to use and share what you're learning.

D. The type of job you have has little to do with your level of drive. It's not what you do but how you do what you do that makes a difference.

E. Drive can turn into blind ambition if you don't have a sense of balance in your life or have only your own interests at heart.

F. Without character, drive can cause you to pursue the wrong things longer and faster.

G. When you feel you've lost your drive it is often because you've become emotionally or physically tired and need to recharge.

H. It's difficult to have drive if you are obsessed and distracted by things you cannot control since you will spend too much time selling out to conditions rather than steering your own destiny.

I. Your manager, spouse, or friends are not the Wizard of Oz who can give you drive, character, or attitude. These are inside jobs. Take responsibility for becoming driven.

Strengthening or Rebuilding Your Drive:

A. You must develop a high enough purpose that ignites your drive. Let me give you a hint here: "Making a living" isn't likely to do the trick. "Making a life for my family and myself" is a much better start.

B. You must narrow your focus since diluted drive results in mediocrity and lots of activity with little accomplishment.

C. You must maintain a sense of balance in life and a selfless attitude. It does you little good to be rich and successful yet sick and alone.

"The real tragedy of the poor is the poverty of their aspirations." —Adam Smith

---

3. Unteachable #3: Talent. A talent is a natural strength that you have inside of you. Think of it as a special wiring that causes certain things to come easy to you and you do them consistently with excellence. Excellence is impossible without talent, but talent, as great as it is, is still only potential. Plenty of people waste their talent because they never get serious about what they want nor develop the discipline to rise above average.

Thoughts on Talent:

A. No one can teach you talent. It is an inside job. Think of talent as God's gift to you so you can make the world a better place.

B. A natural tendency is to ignore your talents because you take them for granted (since things come so easy to you) and spend more time on your weaknesses instead. This is a mistake since you will never become great at what you do by working on weaknesses. Working on weaknesses can get you by, but developing your strengths is what makes you great.

C. Key talent areas in sales include but are not limited to:

(1) **Ego drive.** This means you have a need to persuade and to win.

(2) Ego strength. This means you can bounce back from rejection quickly.

(3) Empathy. This means you are able to read people, sense their emotions, and adjust your style to fit them and their needs.

Strategies to Develop Your Talent:

A. Identify your talents and begin to consciously spend more time on these areas of strength.

B. Stay disciplined in your daily routine because talent can tend to make you lazy (since certain things come so easy to you) and cause you to let up.

C. Continue to raise the bar for yourself in an effort to stimulate your drive and unleash the talent within you.

D. Stay away from unproductive activities and people who diminish your talent.

E. Practice. Talent is only potential, and it must be developed, focused, and refined.

"Practicing a skill is just as important as making a sale. The sale will make you a living but the skill will make you a fortune." —Jim Rohn

---

If you are unsure as to what your talents are or if you have the right talents to succeed in sales, you must spend serious time with honest self-evaluation to help you with this. Otherwise, you'll spend your career and your life running in circles. Our company has an online assessment that helps you evaluate your own and other's strengths in sales. If you happen to be in charge of hiring or training a sales team, e-mail Eric Samuelson at eric@learntolead.com, or give him a call at 804-798-3355, and tell him you'd like an online tour of the Anderson Profile. The insight and coaching it provides to help you hire and develop a sales team will blow you away!

"Attitude is the 'John the Baptist' of your life. It goes before you telling the world, 'He's coming! He's coming!'" —John Maxwell

---

4. **Unteachable #4: Attitude.** You may assume that because I write and speak about motivational matters that my attitude is naturally great and that I run around pumped up all the time. If so, your assumption couldn't be more wrong. Just like any other discipline, I have to work on my attitude daily. I start early in the morning with a regimen of inspirational reading that includes two daily devotionals, filling out a gratitude journal for the things that went right the day before, and reading a chapter of Proverbs. Whenever I get in a hurry and skip this routine I can tell and so can those who know me best. I also have learned to avoid negative, whiney people so they don't annoy, distract, or influence me. This has been particularly difficult over the years because at one time the worst offenders were in my own family. I watch very little television, see few movies, and don't read a daily newspaper. Instead, I get my information about what's happening around the world at select Web sites that present the news objectively. Even with these efforts I often find myself too judgmental, irritable, and impatient—especially while in Los Angeles traffic or while suffering fools at the many airports I pass through. Just like you, I'm a work in progress and

can look back over the years and feel good about the steps forward I've made. At the same time, as I reflect on each day, I am humbled by how far I still have to go. The lesson here is that building an attitude takes constant awareness, hard work, and resolve. And since it will drastically affect your income, sales success, relationships, reputation, and fulfillment with life overall, it may be time to take a closer look at yours and what it is doing for you or against you.

Thoughts on Attitude:

A. Other people as well as your manager may be able to help alter your mood from day to day but no one can teach you or change your prevailing attitude. If you've always been a "yeah but," glass is half-empty person, nothing anyone else can do will change your state for long. Only you can help yourself out of this misery.

B. While you cannot help what happens to you, you are still responsible for choosing a productive response to what happens. Attitude is a choice. When you get up in the morning you have a choice of saying, "Good morning God!" or "Good God! Morning!" Make the right choice.

C. Your attitude comes under siege every day and thus you must do something deliberately to fortify it. Oftentimes your attitude comes under attack long before you're at work: negative news stories, an unhappy spouse or kid, or the driver who cuts you off in traffic and extends a choice finger to indicate that you are "number one." This is why reviewing daily goals, listening to motivational material, and hanging around with positive people is mandatory for fortifying your attitude. Just as when you walk into a dark room you are unable to drive the darkness out until you let in the light, you cannot drive the darkness out of your mind until you fill it with light.

D. Attitude, like any other discipline, will not take care of itself. It's like a muscle that must be strengthened and is formed by the sum of your minute-by-minute, hour-by-hour, day-in, and day-out decisions.

SOBs will challenge your attitude. They will put you to the test. This is why it's vital that you are mentally prepared for worst-case scenarios every day. And when they do get your attitude off track you must have the presence of mind and discipline to be able to shake it off and change your state back to where you are effective and vital.

E. Anyone can have a great attitude when things are going well. The sign of emotional maturity is keeping a good attitude when they are not. Don't be a fair-weather salesperson who can only smile or be positive when things are going your way. The fact is that in most sales professions you will have more slow days than great days, so you must learn to manage your moods or you'll get overwhelmed.

F. Sales experts estimate that 80% of your success in sales is a direct result of your attitude. This is one reason in my book, *Selling Above the Crowd: 365 Strategies for Sales Excellence* (1999), I devoted an entire chapter to the subject of attitude. The importance of attitude is proof why product knowledge experts and veteran salespeople heavy on skills and short on temperament often get outsold by new salespeople who know far less but are powered forward by a contagious attitude.

Nine Strategies to Improve Your Attitude:

1. **Remove yourself from the presence of negative people and situations.** One of the hardest truths you must learn in sales and in life is that there are some people along the way that you must give up in order to go up. At one time you may have shared the same values with these people, but you grew and they didn't. You have a choice: Let them drag you down to their level, or lift yourself to a higher level and in many cases leave them behind in the process. It used to be that people would try to keep up with the Jones' but now it's just cheaper for them to talk you out of it.

"I can tell more about a man, not by his speech, but by the company he keeps." —Martin Luther King Jr.

"The books you read and the people you associate with will determine where you are in life five years from now." —Charles "Tremendous" Jones

---

2. **Focus on what you can control.** You may not be able to control who you get as prospects, but you can control how you respond to the stubborn, obnoxious, belligerent customer. Overall, getting distracted by things you cannot control takes you off your game. By investing your energy into the aspects of your job that you can control, you build your attitude by accepting responsibility and refusing to become a victim. This can't help

but boost your self-esteem and your results. Which response do you choose when you lose a deal or when customer traffic is slow? Take a look at the following.

Examples of Uncontrollable Situations and Potential Responses:

Situation 1: You just lost a deal. **Potential Responses:** (a) tell everyone else about it, (b) pout a while and feel sorry for yourself, (c) talk about what an SOB the "flakey," "stroke" customer is, (d) know that based on the laws of numbers the "no" you just got moved you one step closer to your next deal and get busy to make it happen.

When you fail to make a deal remember S.W.S.W.S.W.S.W.: "Some will, some won't, so what, someone's waiting!" And then get on with life!

Situation 2: Customer traffic is slow. You haven't had a prospect in 2 days. **Potential Responses:** (a) join the huddle of other whiners and talk about how tough this year is going to be; (b) blame the advertising, your inventory, the weather, manager, or economy; (c) discipline yourself to begin contacting past customers and ask for referrals, follow-up all current deals, start calling the prospect lists you have stuffed in your file cabinet, or go out and prospect for fresh business.

Great salespeople never complain about a lack of traffic because they take responsibility for creating their own.

3. **Read or listen to motivational material—preferably early in the day.** Turn off the R-rated disc jockey every once in a while on the way to work and put in a

CD that will help you build your attitude, self-esteem, and skill level.

4. **Set goals and develop a life purpose that motivates you.** People with lousy attitudes normally don't have much worth fighting for, namely goals and purpose. Thus, it's easy to stay down, become apathetic, and give up.

5. **Carefully guard your inner dialogue.** What do you say when you talk to yourself? Sadly, many people wouldn't talk to their worst enemies the way they talk to themselves. With junk like, "I'm never going to make it," "I can't pay my bills," "I'm going to get fired," or "I just cannot sell that type of customer," you can talk yourself into a depression. Stop putting yourself down! Negative self-talk in sales becomes a self-fulfilling prophecy. Program your subconscious with thoughts of possibility, not impossibility.

6. **Don't make it "all about you." Do something for others.** This takes the focus off your own woes and elevates your self-worth, which fires up your attitude, and the good things you do for others tend to come back to you. As paradoxical as it sounds, giving starts the receiving process.

7. **Maintain your integrity in all situations.** You may fool others but you cannot fool yourself, and every time you do something out of alignment with your values or contrary to what you know is right you diminish yourself. The good news is that the opposite is also true.

8. **Always give your best effort.** Even if things don't turn out the way you'd like, you'll feel better about yourself if you know down deep that you did all you could. The bad news is that the opposite is also true. Regardless of the front you put up for others to see, the way you really feel about yourself greatly impacts your performance. As

Jim Rohn said, "Every time you do less than you can you become less than you are." Master trainer and motivator Zig Ziglar summed it up well when he said, "You cannot perform consistently in a manner inconsistent with how you see yourself."

9. **Don't take rejection personally.** Unless you do something really offensive or stupid, a customer rarely rejects you personally; he or she rejects your process, your product, or your price. So don't make it all about you. Most of us get turned down for something every day. I could paper the walls in my home twice over with all the rejection slips I've received over the years for book ideas alone—much less sales I've lost. You're not expected to like rejection. In fact, if you do, you may require therapy. But you are expected to deal with rejection productively by learning from it and taking the lesson gleaned out on your next customer. Besides, if you cannot handle rejection, you've picked a peculiar way to make a living because it is a big part of the selling profession.

"'No' is engagement, not rejection." —Author, Speaker Brian Tracy

---

Review of the Unteachables:

Commit to one action step in each of these areas to develop the unteachables that you must take responsibility for. Be honest with yourself. Most people don't suffer because they can't fix their problems. They suffer because they can't see them or because they know they're there but refuse to look at them. And they can't see them because they're mostly looking in the wrong places: everywhere but in the mirror.

1. Character.
2. Drive.
3. Talent.
4. Attitude.

Sharpen Up by Doubling Up!

You can't grow your career bigger on the outside than you grow on the inside. To get more than you've got you must become more than you are. The "becoming" has to happen first. The following are five ways to sharpen up by doubling up and then going up.

1. Double your knowledge. If you want to double your sales you'll have to double your knowledge and upgrade your skills: selling skills, time management skills, and the like. To paraphrase Jim Rohn, the business will be better when you get better, and you get better when you go to work on yourself. Never wish it were easier; wish you were better!

"Don't chase money. Chase the right skills, habits, and attitude and the money will chase you." —Jim Rohn

---

How many books, CDs, or tapes on sales or motivation did you read or listen to last year? (Please note I didn't ask how many you bought, borrowed, or had given to you. I asked how many you actually read or listened to.) The good news is that if you didn't compile a very long list it won't be hard to double your knowledge this year. Make no mistake about it: Time and experience doesn't automatically equate to growth. Growth is not automatic. Death is automatic. Growth must be intentional. Now I hope you're not sitting there thinking up excuses as to why you don't have time to read, practice, or listen to motivational or instructional material. How many hours of television do you watch each week? Now multiply it by 52 and put the answer here: _____. How many *days* does this equate to? Do you still believe you don't have time to work on the craft of selling?

To go up you must give something up: trivial conversations, mindless hours surfing the Web or watching television. This will take change, and change always involves a loss of some kind. You must let go of old ways to experience the new. And don't forget that the objective of learning is action not the warehousing of knowledge. Knowing is nothing. Life rewards action. You can't just sit and think your way to the next level. Somewhere along the line you need to do something with what you learn.

"Mindless television and radio is an income suppressant." —Zig Ziglar

---

2. Double your discipline. Discipline is a morale builder. When you make yourself do the right things consistently you feel better about yourself. Without discipline, doubling your knowledge will be irrelevant because even if you do get started on a personal growth program you'll become inconsistent.

A. You develop discipline by growing up. You make yourself do the things you know are important even when you don't feel like doing them. In other words, you stop doing only what you feel like doing and do what is right.

B. You develop discipline by holding yourself accountable and, if necessary, getting someone else to hold you accountable as well. If you know you have to answer for failing to do what you've committed to do, you're more likely to do what you said you'd get done.

C. You develop discipline by holding in your mind the future picture of what you want your career and life to look like. Discipline bridges the gap between your goals and actually achieving them. When you're tempted to skip a discipline, replay the picture of what you want your future to look like and that image will help pull you through the tendency to be lazy or complacent today. If you can't think past today, you'll never create your ideal tomorrow.

Here's some good news: Even if you're the most undisciplined slob known to man, there is hope for you! Discipline is not something you're born with it is something you can develop. After all, the doctor doesn't walk out of the delivery room and say, "Well, well, that is quite the disciplined baby in there."

3. Double your internal focus. Your internal focus relates to the areas in your life over which you have total control: attitude, discipline, work ethic, your level of self-motivation, where you spend your time and with whom you spend it, and your character choices.

4. Double your activity rate. One way to double your sales to SOBs is to double the rate of productive activities you engage in. The key is to be proactive. Your activity rate is unlikely to double as you sit at your desk and wait for something to happen.

"Keep on going and the chances are you will stumble onto something, perhaps when you least expect it. I have never heard of anyone stumbling onto something sitting down." —Charles Kettering

A. What could you do to double the number of outside prospects you find on your own rather than waiting for sales calls or customers to come and find you?

B. How many appointments do you average each week? If you don't know you can't very well double the amount. But if you know your appointment numbers you can set daily goals that double your current number. You can double this number by either making more calls, becoming more effective with the calls you're already making, or a combination of both.

C. What impact would it have on your income if you doubled the number of referrals you're currently getting? Again, first you need to track and know your current numbers and then start asking more people to expand your pipeline of prospects. Many salespeople get so few referrals that doubling the number is a cinch. Set weekly goals for referrals, and don't stop until you get them. And don't be afraid to ask. Instead, you should be afraid of a lousy paycheck. The more friends and referrals you get to sell, the fewer SOBs you'll have to spend time with. More about this in Chapter 7.

5. Double your devotion to balance in your life. If the topic of finding more balance in your life sounds soft to you, it's time to wake up. Living your life out of balance will eventually destroy your career, to say nothing of your health, relationships, and spiritual well-being.

Which cycle sounds most like your life? You work such long hours and days that you're rarely at home with your family. Thus, when you are there it is stressful because there's a lot to do and little time to do it in and you catch grief from the people at home because they don't get to see you enough. This creates stress that you bring right back into the workplace with you, making you even less effective. As a result, you'll have to spend even more time on the job trying to make a living. It's a *vicious* cycle. However, the better you get at work the less time you have to spend there and the more time you can spend having and enjoying a life. This sense of well-being also follows you back into the workplace and makes you even more effective on the job. It is a cycle of *virtue*.

"Don't get so busy with production that you ignore your capacity to produce." —Stephen Covey

---

A. This is why you must devote yourself to the other four areas in this "Sharpen Up by Doubling Up" section. They all make you more effective on the job and put into motion the cycle of virtue that increases productivity even more.

B. Remember that balance must be pursued. It doesn't just ensue, and it won't just find you. Anything worth having must be chased. You may never find yourself in perfect balance. And that's not even the point. The point is that you can't afford to get too far out of balance in any area of your life because the let up in that sector will affect all others. Successful sales and successful living mandates that you make continual adjustments to get your life into further balance.

From time to time you may hear someone complain that they've been working too long and hard and are suffering from burnout. All things considered, that comment is a crock. I know plenty of people who work long and hard and never burn out, and I'm sure that you do as well. Over the years I have found that people who "burn out" in sales don't necessarily work longer or harder than those that don't. Because they live their lives out of balance, they suffer enormous stress. And it's that stress that causes the burnout.

"Fatigue makes cowards of us all." —Vince Lombardi

SOB Summary for Chapter 2: Toughen Up; Sharpen Up; Grow Up & Go Up!

When you reexamine the principles presented in "Toughen Up; Sharpen Up; Grow Up & Go Up" you're likely to agree that each principle is designed to improve your self-esteem, self-image, and self-confidence, which in turn lead to more belief in self. It's hard to put a price on this belief, especially when you're dealing with challenging, difficult customers, some of whom may try to make you feel small, insignificant, or stupid. Even when you do fail to make a sale it won't affect you as much when your belief in self is intact. As you become more confident in who you are you will be less concerned with the opinions of others or with stumbling blocks along the way. Key takeaways from Chapter 2 are:

1. Understand the four unteachables vital to sales success and take personal responsibility for developing these traits. You will never be great at selling difficult customers on the outside until you're what you should be on the inside.

   A. Character.

   B. Drive.

   C. Talent.

   D. Attitude.

2. Sharpen up by doubling up your:

   A. Knowledge. Work harder on yourself and the SOBs will be a piece of cake.

   B. Discipline. Make yourself do the right things even when you don't feel like it.

   C. Activity rate. Stay in motion and make things happen.

   D. Devotion to balance in life. The better life you have away from work, the more effective you'll be on the job.

3 | Don't Just Be Better, Be Different!

Let's Start with Straight Talk

As much as most people and businesses like to think that they're different or better than a competitor, it's simply not the case. Take airlines for instance. If you couldn't see the logo and were sitting in row 20 of a 737, when you consider the quality of the seat, surroundings, food, service, and attitude of the flight attendants, would you be able to tell with whom you were flying? Probably not. This is one of the key reasons most airline fares are so similar. It's called the Law of Differentiation, which says that the less you differentiate yourself from others, the more price sensitive people become, but the more you differentiate yourself from others, the less price sensitive people become. You should memorize that law. Here is some good news: If you're both different and better than your competition, customers—and yes, even

SOBs—see more value in you and are willing to pay for it. But if you look, sound, and act like every other salesperson in your field and represent your products in the same mundane manner, people will become increasingly price sensitive because, since everything else is pretty much the same, the primary differentiator between you and your competition becomes how cheap they can get what you sell.

The Danger of Blending into the Crowd

The lesson for you, as a sales professional, is this: If you keep getting beat up on price by most of the SOBs you try to sell and dropping your price has become your number one tool for closing a deal, it is probably because you're just like every other average, ho-hum, boring, long-winded, and forgettable salesperson these challenging clients have dealt with throughout their life. And, yes, what you sell is important. But keep this in mind: Your number one competitor is not another product or service. It is the other salesperson peddling these things. It's you against them and you need an edge to emerge as the winner.

A Lesson from Larry

Larry Matney understands the Law of Differentiation. In fact, he is unforgettable. As a result, he gets top dollar for his products and earns repeat customers who religiously stop by his store, Gregory's, in the Dallas Galleria Shopping Center.

My wife and I met Larry when we flew to Dallas to attend a friend's wedding. Since the Galleria was just a short distance from our hotel we decided to pass some time the night before the gala looking around its three floors of fine shops. As we passed by Gregory's, a unique and elaborate pair of cowboy boots caught my wife's eye. Rhonda had never owned cowboy boots and had no plans to buy these. She just wanted to take a closer look. As she picked up a boot to look it over, Larry approached her with a broad smile, introduction and with more enthusiasm than Paula Deen has for buttermilk biscuits. Rhonda quickly told Larry that she was just looking but before we knew it, Larry had built instant rapport with his Texas charm and had her laughing, sitting down and trying on the boots, while he sat on the floor in front of her casually issuing orders for the sales staff to bring certain styles and sizes for a tryout. When Rhonda got up to walk in the boots Larry asked how they felt and when she replied that they seemed a bit unsteady, Larry assured her she'd get used to them and to prove his point, took her hand and began waltzing with her across the floor while the entire sales force looked on with a mix of disbelief and awe. I was laughing at the spectacle until I realized we were probably going to end up buying that fancy footwear, which I suspected would cost a small fortune.

We found out later that Larry was the owner of Gregory's and that whenever he stopped by his store he personally waited on customers and put on a sales clinic for his entire team to learn from. Before long, Rhonda was paying more for a pair of boots than she had ever paid for a pair of shoes in her life. And we both knew that she was unlikely to ever wear them. So why'd she pay so much for something that was likely to gather dust in a closet? Larry was different and so were his boots. He transformed a typical sales encounter into an event and at that point the price didn't matter. When you're in the presence of genius, you just say, "I'll take it."

Consider the following "Law of the Edge" and then adapt the four strategies given to become different and better than your competition to put this law to work for you:

The Law of the Edge: The horse that wins a race by a nose wins 10 times more money than the second place horse. This doesn't mean the winning horse was 10 times better. Instead, it shows the power a slight edge over your competitor has on your personal success.

Use Rapport as Your Differentiator and Your Edge:

1. Take the time to build rapport with your prospects even when they seem tough, coarse, or impatient. "Rapport" is defined by Oxford Dictionary as "a harmonious and understanding relationship between people." Thus whatever you do during the sales process that increases harmony and understanding, however small or insignificant it may seem, is helping you build the rapport necessary to make a prospect comfortable enough with you to buy what you're selling. Oftentimes, going right for the throat without taking the time to build rapport is the surest way to convert a normal prospect into an SOB. The good news for you is that the majority of your competitors are lousy at building rapport. They either do it poorly or don't do it all. Look at the rapport-building skills you'll learn in this section as a way to differentiate yourself.

Building rapport may come naturally for you but it didn't for me. I was a bottom-liner as a salesperson and lousy at small talk. Before I sold cars I sold insurance door-to-door, where I had to talk fast and get right down to business. Foolishly, I applied this same sales technique when selling automobiles. Of course, I blamed my customers for not buying from me. Obviously, they were not serious, were tightwads, or were just out killing time. I'd go home and complain to my wife about all the SOBs I was meeting in the car business. This was almost as tough as going door-to-door. Thankfully, a veteran salesperson took me aside one day and told me, "Anderson, you're scaring your customers by moving so fast. Go out there and talk about anything other than a car deal for the first few minutes. You've got to get them to like you, and right now, they don't." I'll always be grateful for that advice. Whether you're a born rapport builder or lousy at it like I was, the following strategies will help you sell more and sell more profitably. In Chapter 8 I'll present five ways to get "in" rapport with your prospect, but we need to lay the following groundwork first with these 11 tips.

Eleven Ways to Build Rapport:

A. Build client rapport by remembering and repeating the client's name throughout the sales process. Remembering the names of others in the buying party also helps you create harmony and build rapport. As egocentric as it may sound, we all like the sound of our name and will remember and appreciate those who take the time to use it.

Three Tips to Remember Names:

(1) Use their name in the same manner they give it to you. For instance, if a prospect tells you their name is James Johnson, don't call him Jim or Jimmy. I go by Dave Anderson, not David. There's nothing wrong with David, I've just asked to be called Dave since the fourth grade. So, after I've introduced myself as Dave and someone calls me David, I consider it as strike one. Three strikes—at the most—and I tend to become an SOB.

(2) Repeat their name right after they give it to you so you make sure you are saying it right. Saying it quickly after the introduction will also help you remember the name. You're better off to get a mistake corrected early than to irritate and distract your customer throughout the process by calling them the wrong thing.

(3) If the name is unusual or difficult to pro-nounce, don't be embarrassed to ask them if you're saying it right. Just say, "I want to make sure I say your name right, is it pronounced as XXXX?" This won't offend most people. In fact, they're more likely to appreciate the fact that you're making an earnest effort to get it right.

B. Mirror the prospect's pace. Speaking or moving at a speed drastically different than that of your prospect creates disharmony and a disconnect between you and the prospect. If you are naturally fast talking and your prospect couldn't win a sprint against a snail, you're going to have to tone it down a tad. On the other hand, if you're the slow-but-steady, methodical type and your prospect is high energy and fleet of foot, you'll need to pick up the pace. I can assure you that your prospect is not interested in having you turn the sales process into a death march.

C. Learn to sell with questions, not just with answers. You build rapport with SOBs by engaging them with questions, not by rambling on with excessive information. If building rapport means you create an understanding with the other person, you must ask questions because people only buy when they feel understood, and the only way you can make them feel understood is by asking questions concerning wants and needs and really listening to the answers.

D. Remember that rapport is not something you stop doing after the first few minutes of the sales process. You must continue to build rapport throughout the sales encounter; otherwise it comes off as a mere formality you went through right before "getting down to business and going for the sale," and SOBs will see right through your transparency. Building rapport is more of a process than a sales step. Oftentimes initial good feelings wear off soon after you establish early rapport if you're not continuing to build harmony and understanding throughout the process. When you do your "two-minute" drill of rapport building and then put your "do or die" game face on, people sense you are disingenuous, an amateur, a phony.

E. Make good eye contact with each person you meet. This technique seems so basic you might wonder why I've included it here. The answer is simple: Too many salespeople still don't have the good manners to pull this off. You also should extend your hand, and if SOB, don't want to shake it they won't, but you should give them the choice. Hold your eye contact throughout the initial introduction. Learn to smile with your eyes. They are the window to who—and where—you are at the moment.

F. For goodness sakes, smile! If you're having a bad day, tough! Your prospects don't want to deal with a grump and could not care less what your problems happen to be. Whining about the day or week you're having is not a viable way to build rapport. It *is* a fast way to become resented or despised by SOBs who happen to have their own problems and don't appreciate you filling their space with negativity. Don't ever resort to becoming one of those sour, dour sales schmucks shuffling around all day looking tortured, annoyed, or confused. These people's attitudes are so dangerous that they should be forced to wear crime scene tape around their head.

G. Discuss noncontroversial topics in order to build rapport. Don't bring up politics or religion unless you're meeting the person at a political fundraiser or church event. The weather and local sporting events are normally safe bets. During an election year, a salesman working for our dealership noticed a political bumper sticker a customer had on his car and decided to use it as an avenue to build rapport. The conversation went something like this:

> SALESPERSON: "Hi there. I see by your sticker that you're pulling for Candidate So and So. I sure like that guy and think he's going to carry this county and the state."
>
> SOON-TO-BE-GONE PROSPECT: Standing with his arm crossed and a scowl as rigid as Mount Rushmore: "This isn't my car. I'm borrowing it from a friend because I just wrecked my Camry and need another one. And I don't like the guy you just mentioned, and I don't really like you either right now. Is there someone else here I can deal with?"

H. Give a sincere compliment. If they have a beautiful office, they're proud of that. When appropriate, acknowledge this and pay them a compliment. If someone is wearing a unique piece of jewelry or carrying an unusual purse, ask about it. This creates harmony and shows an interest in more than simply making the sale and getting their dollars. Don't cross the line and be nosy like the clothing salesperson at a men's store at Caesar's Palace who, while trying to sell me a new leather jacket, noticed my watch and guessed what it "set me back." I told him that his guess was pretty close and because of that I couldn't afford the jacket he was showing me. Ignorant, poorly mannered salespeople can turn me into an SOB, how about you?

I. Don't talk too much about yourself. This only adds value if your prospects need sleep. I can sum up the approach many salespeople take while they think they're building rapport: too much information! I once had a shoe salesperson apologize for being a little sluggish as he explained that he'd been "stopped up" for about a week. This remark did succeed in distracting me from the price, but it raised a new and greater concern that he might explode.

J. You can build rapport with even the most "bottom line" SOBs by getting them to talk about themselves or their business. Even the stodgiest ogre doesn't seem to mind talking about themselves: what they do, how well they do it, where they've been, and what they've accomplished. Put your ego aside and get them bragging a bit; it goes a long way to building rapport.

K. Don't excuse yourself to take phone calls, answer pages, or talk on your cell phone. This tells your prospects that whoever is calling, for whatever reason, is more important than they are and that they'll have to take a backseat to the unknown. Do this to the wrong prospect and you'll have an instant SOB. Abuse even the friendliest customers in this manner and they'll politely go somewhere else.

In an age when employees of large and small organizations alike routinely treat customers like interruptions, where they install phone systems that dehumanize people by forcing them to converse with computers rather than speak with a human being, is it any wonder that so many customers have come to expect the worst when trying to do business and have become less loyal to brands and businesses as a result? In fact, service has become so poor today that when you find a cheerful, helpful, knowledgeable salesperson you're tempted to drug test him. This epidemic of unprofessionalism and indifference is your opportunity to set yourself apart and earn both normal and SOB customers for life by being better and different. Taking the time to connect with the customer by building rapport, asking the right questions, maintaining a genial demeanor, and focusing like a laser on their needs before going for the jugular will both tame tried and tested SOBs and prevent the conversion of normal customers to that sorry state.

2. Use appropriate humor to differentiate yourself and make yourself more likable. According to sales trainer and author, Jeffrey Gitomer, "If I can get my prospect or customer to laugh, I can get him or her to buy. . . . So can you." Using appropriate humor in sales takes creativity and finesse, but it is a great avenue through which you differentiate yourself from the horde of other bland, boring, wind bag salespeople who talk themselves out of more sales than they ever make. Contrary to what you may believe, stubborn, obnoxious, and belligerent customers often will respond more favorably to humor because it makes you different, pleasant, and even fun, which can stop a normal customer from converting to an SOB and melt a dyed-in-the-wool Grinch faster than a Christmas chorus from Whoville.

Seven Tips for Using Appropriate Humor to Make More Sales:

A. Understand what using appropriate humor doesn't mean. There's a big difference between being humorous and silly, between lightening up the customer and offending them. Though it should go without saying, I'd be remiss if I didn't point out what I *don't* mean by selling with humor.

(1) It doesn't mean telling off-color jokes.

(2) It doesn't mean using off-color language.

(3) It doesn't mean you must try too hard to be funny.

(4) It doesn't mean you make fun of others, only yourself.

(5) It doesn't mean you go from being humorous to being just plain goofy.

B. Use appropriate humor early on to break the ice and build rapport. For instance, when you're in the rapport-building stage and find that you're dealing with someone who is a native to the city where you're selling—and you are not—find a way to weave in that while you're not from here originally, you "got here as fast as you could."

You can also use this phrase when someone asks how long you've been in the business you're in: "Well, I used to be in the fertilizer business, but when I found out how great the car business was I got into as fast as I could. I figured it would be more fun to sell cars than manure."

Note: Do not say this to a customer until you are sure he or she doesn't sell fertilizer for a living!

If you used to sell anything door to door you can also find a place to add: "When I sold widgets door to door I got two orders from every stop I made: Get out and stay out!"

C. Use appropriate humor when you make a mistake. When you've told a customer something that ends up being wrong or when you make some other big/obvious mistake throughout the sales process, say something like, "Well you must feel truly honored to be dealing with the dumbest/most forgetful/dingiest/most uncoordinated/clumsiest salesperson in town. I believe that if I visited a mind reader today they'd only charge me half price." This type of self-deprecation resonates with others and makes even the most hardcore SOB cut you some slack and puts him on your side.

Using appropriate humor can take a serious thing, like a mistake, spilling a drink on a prospect, forgetting their name, etc., and turn it into an asset that will help you close the sale.

D. Use appropriate humor when the customer says "no" to relieve tension and move you closer to the sale. "Mr. Prospect, as strange as this may sound, it's good to hear you say 'no.' I just got back from a sales class that taught me that 80% of the sales are made after five "no's." So, if we can find four other things for you to say 'no' to, we ought to be pretty close to making the deal."

Then follow up with something like:

"Seriously now, if there were one thing holding you back from moving forward today, what is it? I should remind you that answering "I don't know" would be our second "no" and move us even closer to the sale, so if you want to get out of here without buying something today, you'll need to be as specific as possible."

E. Use appropriate humor when dealing with customer problems or complaints. When a prospect is emotionally charged up about a problem or complaint, the last thing you want to do is escalate the issue by saying things like "It's not my job," "It's not my fault," "You'll have to see so and so," or by copping an attitude and becoming indifferent, indolent, or idiotic. Instead, depending on the problem's severity, say something like the following and use the right tone and pace:

"Mr. Prospect, first of all let me thank you for not shouting at me, hitting me, or sending a Soprano to break my legs because, if something like this had happened to me, I don't think I'd be handling it as well as you are. (You can say this sincerely even if they're being obnoxious because it will slow them down and help take the fight out of the situation.) Then proceed with: "Let's see what *we* can do to fix this right away."

F. Use humorous analogies to add spice and life to your presentations. If I could corral most of the sales presentations I've seen over the years, bottle them up and sell them as sleeping aids, I could retire tomorrow. Humorous presentations differentiate you, make you memorable, and loosen up SOBs faster than a bottle of Fibercon. Think about the features and products you present and come up with phrases like these to add spice and life to them.

"Mr. Prospect, this engine will go from 0–60 faster than granny can shout, 'Bingo'!"

"Mr. Prospect, this trunk is so big that if you look long enough you might find Jimmy Hoffa."

"Mr. Prospect, I'd like to inform you that this car rides smoother than most Bentleys. I'd like to inform you of this, but I can't—but it does have the best ride in its class."

"Mr. Prospect, advertising on our station will draw a bigger crowd than the outhouse at a chili cook off."

G. Use appropriate humor when you follow-up with working and sold customers.

(1) If you fax information to a prospect, use a unique and humorous cover sheet to stand out from the crowd. Have it say something like:

Please deliver this message at once to the Very Important Person Named Above

If you are not this person, please don't be nosy and read what I'm sending.

My phone number is: 818-735-9979

My fax number is: 818-735-0299

Hurry up!

Author and sales trainer Jeffrey Gitomer, from whom I learned this technique[1], says he gets about five comments per week from his version of a humorous fax sheet. It makes him memorable and grabs the prospect's attention, and both those things help make more sales.

(2) When you leave a voice mail, come up with something light and different that will help you stand out and increase the odds the prospect will call you back:

"Mr. Jones, this is Dave Anderson, and I'm sure you're busy but I knew you would probably be horribly disappointed in me if I didn't call you back right away and try to set another appointment for you to look at our product. And there is no way I ever want to let any of my customers down by making them believe that I've forgotten them or didn't take them seriously. Please call me at 818-735-9999 so I know that you know I'm still thinking of you and want your business more than anyone else in the business."

Or in an instance where you've called a customer

back and left numerous messages that have gone unanswered, you can try something like the following
with just the right tone and inflection. After all, at
this stage you have little to lose and much to gain by
being bold and a bit humorous at the same time:

"Mr. Jones, this is Dave Anderson again, and I
have some new information to share with you. Please
either call me back or swear out a restraining order
because I won't rest until I have you involved with
our product."

**3. Differentiate yourself from other salespeople by
learning how to justify your price.** Lowering the price
should be your last resort in order to make a sale, not the first
offer out of your mouth. However, if you don't learn to justify your price, you have no choice but to drop it. The good
news is that the better you get at justifying what you ask,
the less often you will have to accept less than you're asking. Salespeople tend to back down when they have a tough
customer and start dropping the price in order to pacify the
SOB. You must renounce this strategy of surrender if you
want to stand out from the crowded field of sales amateurs
and earn what you deserve in sales.

The following four strategies are specifically designed
for customers trading in cars, boats, RVs, motorcycles, office
or manufacturing equipment, etc. or purchasing products or
services that are limited in supply. It also works well for anyone financing a purchase.

**A. Use the "maintenance close" to justify making
a higher payment.** The maintenance close educates a
customer to what the "real payment" is on their current
product. For instance, if they paid $1,200 in repairs last
year for tires, engine, and brake work and their payment
to the bank is $350, then their *real* payment is $450 per

month ($350 to the bank and another $100 per month just to keep the clunker running). This perspective comes in handy when you have a stubborn customer who wants to keep his payment at the same $350 he's paying now and you present him with one that is $100 per month higher. Rather than lower your price to get closer to the $350, you can *justify* your price by reminding Mr. Stubborn that you're not asking any more than he's already paying for a product he no longer wants.

B. Use the "longer you wait the worse it gets" close. Since the price of new vehicles go up and the value of trade-ins go down, putting off a purchase because the price is too high is a flawed strategy. A prospect is better off paying the higher price now since terms will only be worse in the future. You might explain it like this:

"Mr. Prospect, you mentioned that you'd like to save more money to put down on this product to keep your payment lower. While that may sound like a good idea, I should point out that your good intentions could actually cost you money. You see, the price of the product you're looking at goes up each year, and it has a rebate that will expire soon. At the same time, the vehicle you're trading in is worth less every month and can really take a hit if it crosses a certain mile threshold or something goes wrong with it mechanically. Unfortunately, when this happens, the longer you wait to purchase the worse things can get. To prevent this from happening, wouldn't it make sense to trade in your vehicle now, since it will never be worth any more than it is today, and lock in the price on this new one before the rebate disappears?"

C. Reduce the difference between the payment you're proposing and the payment the customer wants to pay to the ridiculous. If you want to sell more SOBs you should incorporate two important phrases into your selling arsenal: "Part of my job is to make this make sense for you" and "Part of my job is to stop you from making a mistake." These are collaborative, non-confrontational words that put you and your customer on the same side. You can use these power phrases when helping a customer justify why he should pay more than he wants or expected to pay. Reducing to the ridiculous is a proven sales technique that many salespeople neglect. It puts higher-than-expected terms in a manner customers can more easily rationalize and feel equipped to handle. For instance, being $60 per month away from what the customer wants may seem insurmountable, but when you reduce it to the ridiculous, it makes sense:

"Mr. Prospect, we're within $60 per month of where you had hoped to be. And I know you said that if we couldn't reach your desired payment that you'd go elsewhere. But part of my job is to make this deal make sense for you and to stop you from making a mistake. There are other products I can sell you that will meet the payment you're looking for, but they wouldn't be what you told me that you'd like. The fact is that you're only $2 per day away from getting what you want and deserve. There must be someplace in your budget where we can find that $2—after all, it's only a coke and bag of chips. It doesn't seem right to pass up our first choice over a daily handful of junk food now does it?"

Please notice how that in each of these scenarios, even while you dealt with customers who didn't want to buy on your terms, you never dropped your price. You justified it. You made it make sense. You got on the side of the customer to prevent them from making a mistake. This differentiates you; it makes you friends; it makes you better; and, very important, it makes you money!

D. Create and use an evidence manual to prove what you tell customers. SOBs can be skeptical. They don't respond well to being told. They want to be shown. An evidence manual is a tool you use to prove what you're saying, distinguish your professionalism, and build value in you, your product, and your company. Most salespeople don't take the time to assemble an evidence manual because it's too much trouble. In other words, because they're lazy. You can do better by considering and acting on these steps that help you make your "case" when selling SOBs.

"As I grow older, I pay less attention to what men say and instead watch what they do."
—Andrew Carnegie

---

(1) What an evidence manual is and contains: A three-ring binder divided into the following sections: product information, copies of customer satisfaction reports (if applicable to your industry) and happy customer letters people have written you, positive press clips on what you sell, personal awards you've earned, etc.

An evidence manual can be assembled over time. It's a continual process, and you should upgrade and update it often. Begin with a few pages and continue to expand with new data. You probably already have much of the contents stuffed in file drawers or notebooks.

(2) How to use an evidence manual: If you have to leave a customer in your office while you check with your manager for sales figures, use words similar to these:

"Ms. Prospect, I'm going to go consult with my manager and see what our figures look like. While I'm gone, page through here and see if you know any of these customers I've sold."

Or,

". . . while I'm gone, take a look at what *Car & Driver* Magazine had to say about the car you want."

Or,

". . . while I go check our inventory, take a look at what *Jewelers World* had to say about the watch you like."

(3) Use it to "stop a customer from making a mistake" when he or she speaks of shopping for a competitive product.

When I was the sales manager for a Toyota dealership we had a stubborn and borderline belligerent customer looking at a Celica. Nothing our sales rep did could close the deal. He was determined to go buy a competitive product from a rival import dealer. Before he left, the salesperson brought the customer by my office so I could thank him for coming in and giving us a shot at his business. After meeting him I told him the following: "Mr. Prospect, I appreciate you stopping by and looking at our product. I understand that we're your second choice and you're on your way to buy XYZ product. Mr. Prospect, part of my job is to make this deal make sense for you and to stop you from making a mistake, so before you make your final decision, I thought you'd like to see what *Consumer Reports* had to say about XYZ." At that point, I showed him our departmental evidence manual with a copy of the magazine page that showed that XYZ was rated as the least reliable car in its class. Old stone face looked like someone had just socked him in the gut. He stared at me, looked back at the evidence manual, and then looked back at me again before plopping down in a chair and saying, "All right. I'll take the Celica."

Needless to say, if rather than showing him the evidence I had said, "Mr. Prospect, before you make your final decision, I should *tell* you what *Consumer Reports* had to say about the XYZ," it wouldn't have been nearly as effective and would probably have sounded like another typical sales line.

"There is a declining world market for words." —Lech Walesa

SOB Summary for Chapter 3: Don't Just Be Better, Be Different!

1. The Law of Differentiation states that the more you differentiate yourself from your competitors the less price sensitive customers become, but the less you differentiate yourself from others the more price-sensitive they become. What makes you different and better? If you can't be specific, compelling, and convincing, prepare yourself for only average paychecks and a lackluster career in sales.

2. Connect with SOBs by establishing common ground and building rapport because it is the fastest technique to converting them to a normal customer. Touch their heart before you ask for their wallet.

3. Use appropriate humor to set you apart from the mob of sales mummies going through the motions each day and turning the sales process into a drag. If you can have fun and make it fun for your prospect, they will remember you, appreciate you, and buy from you.

4. Dropping your price should be the strategy of last resort, even when selling to the stubborn, obnoxious, and belligerent. Learn the phrases and techniques that will help you justify your price and maintain a maximum profit for your trouble.

5. An evidence manual takes a little time and effort but it will set you apart in your field. You'll also be equipped to prove what you have to say to the toughest customers rather than count on them to accept your word. An evidence manual makes you different, better, and more confident, and all three traits are essential to selling more SOBs.

4

Take the Fight Out of the Sales Process!

Let's Start with Straight Talk

Without meaning to, you can pick a fight or create a fight in the sales process from the moment a prospect sees you (or hears your voice on the telephone) until the time you try and close the deal. One thing you must remember is that you can't win a fight with a customer. They always get to have the last words, and those words can range from "no" to "I'll go elsewhere" to "shove it." Without meaning to, you can create buyer's resistance and resentment with your attitude, grooming and dress, deficient skills and knowledge, as well as by things you cannot help: your gender, age, accent, or ethnicity. You may declare that it is unfair to do nothing wrong and still have a buyer resist doing business with you just because he's an SOB with an attitude, a prejudice, a chip on his shoulder the size of a lumber yard, or some other bias against someone who looks, talks, and acts like you. You're right, it may be unfair. But much about life is unfair. I personally don't think it's fair for unemployed louts with more cigarettes in their mouth than teeth to win the lottery with tickets they bought from welfare check proceeds while hard working widows raising three kids can't pay their bills, but it happens and the "system" could not care less about my perception of fairness. Being "fair" isn't the point. Making the sale is the point. So put on your thick skin, grow up a bit, and let's talk about some ways to avoid doing or saying something stupid during the sales process that would create tension and how to defuse a fight an SOB seems intent on picking with you when it's not your fault.

Thirteen Strategies for Taking the Fight Out of the Sales Process

First let's cover the areas that you can control:

1. Look/sound like you actually want to be at work. Prospects are irritated early on in the sales process by salespeople apparently indifferent to whether or not they make the sale. If you tick them off early on, SOBs will not buy from you out of spite, even if they really need or want what you're selling. If you're having a bad day, I can promise you that no one wants to hear about it, especially people trying to spend money with you. You'll never get much sympathy from an SOB by whining and crying about how tough things are. They're more likely to despise you for your weakness and kick you when you're down.

If I might recommend one phrase you never use when a customer asks how you're doing, it is the victim-driven whiney drivel and sobbing snivel known as "I'm hanging in there." Have you ever given any thought to just how pathetic "I'm hanging in there" sounds? In a profession as great as sales, in a country as great as ours, in times as abundant as these, if "I'm hanging in there" is the best you can do when someone asks your state you'd be better off to say nothing. As it says in Proverbs, it is better to remain silent and be thought a fool than to open your mouth and remove any doubt. If you'd like to gain some perspective on how well you're really doing and see people who are truly hanging in there, I recommend you visit a severe burn victim, an Alzheimer's ward, or a veteran's hospital.

"It is impossible to antagonize and influence at the same time." —John Knox

---

2. Avoid too much hype in your presentation. Prospects are insulted and annoyed by exaggerated and general claims of what your product or service can do. Once they begin to doubt your integrity and sense that sensationalism is supplanting facts early on in the sales process, they will continue to doubt you all the way up until they leave without buying what you're selling.

3. Don't knock the competition. Learn enough about your product and the competition's product to intelligently answer questions and provide comparisons. Again, avoid using exaggerations or generalizations: "They make very unreliable cars," "Their mortgage rates are always higher than average," or "No one listens to their radio station."

4. Don't talk down to anyone in the buying party. This especially includes women, children, and gatekeepers. When you alienate these influencers early on in the sales process, stick a fork in you because you're done. John Maxwell suggests that one way to value people is to mentally visualize a "10" on everyone's forehead and treat them accordingly, make good eye contact, and speak from your heart. If it is your custom to shake hands with a prospect and his or her family is with them, extend your hand to everyone—and yes, that includes the four year old with a gob of gook caked around his left nostril.

5. Don't sprinkle your presentation with profanity, off-color stories, or remarks. In case you missed this when I discussed a similar topic in Chapter 1, profanity, sex, politics, jokes, and any potentially offensive anecdote should be left out of your conversations with a prospect, even if you think they feel the same way you feel. These are emotional issues and once you trigger them your prospect is likely to become so distracted or get so worked up he or she can't concentrate on the sales process. The result is an instant SOB. In fact, if you think it's funny or somehow appropriate to "lightly curse" or make suggestive remarks to a prospect, then one day you can expect to find a message at the receptionist's desk that reads something like this: "Your proctologist called. They found your head."

6. Don't begin your investigative wants and needs analysis too soon. Too soon is before you've established enough common ground and trust so that the prospect feels comfortable opening up to you. By jumping into your investigative sequence too soon in the presentation, you can give the appearance of "going for the throat" and caring little for the prospect like I discussed in the building rapport section of the last chapter. This doesn't mean you engage in lengthy, trivial small talk, wasting your time and the prospect's. Build rapport by getting the prospect to talk about himself or herself and their business. This is an especially effective way to loosen up difficult customers.

"Seek first to understand, then to be understood."
—Stephen Covey

---

7. Don't argue with prospects, even if you're right. There's a difference between arguing and persuading. Arguing is when you get defensive and go on the offensive too far, too fast. You can win every argument, be 100% right, and still get 0% of the sales because ultimately the customer gets to win every single argument by leaving without buying. When someone says something that is wrong or that you disagree with, say something like this:

"Well, that is one way to look at it. Have you also thought about looking at it this way . . . ?"

As an old adage goes, never argue publicly with a fool. Spectators can't tell the difference.

8. Avoid the words "that's not my job" or any variation thereof when explaining to a customer why you cannot accommodate their request or why you don't know something. These can be fighting words. Customers—most notably SOBs—want to do things their way, not your way, and quite frankly they don't want to hear your excuses they just want results. Thus, you must skillfully handle requests that are not within your realm by bypassing or handing them off without uttering a sales-killing phrase, such as "that's not my job" or "that's my manger's job." Instead say something like,

"My general manager would know about that. Why don't you let me check with him for you?"

9. Plant seeds early on in the sales process that lower the customer's defenses and show the prospect that you're different. Adapt the following words to fit your style and situation and use them early on in the presentation:

"Mrs. Prospect, during the presentation if you have questions, please ask me. If I don't know the answer I'll find out. Also, if I'm going too fast just tell me, and if I show you something you're not interested in let me know and I'll move on to something that works better for you."

By laying out these very collaborative, nonconfrontational ground rules early on in the sales process you create trust, enhance rapport, remove potential confrontation, and differentiate yourself all at the same time.

10. Know that prospects will judge your grooming, your dress, your piercings and tattoos, your smoking habit, your exotic hair style, and the pants that sag down and expose your Mickey Mouse boxer shorts. "Not fair" you may declare, but in the real world people judge you by all these things. Right or wrong, it happens all the time. Most prospects, and especially SOBs, like to feel that they're dealing with a serious professional and, even though you may possess great skills and knowledge, many people will have a hard time getting past "you" in order to listen to what you have to say. In fact, before you even say your first words, they may have taken one look at you and convinced themselves that somewhere a village is missing its idiot. Customers could not care less about what type of statement you're trying to make, how unique and individualistic you're trying to be, or any other issues that might cause you to mutilate your body, dress like a slob, or fail to bathe or groom properly. And if you smoke, I can assure you that customers don't want to see you smoking, they don't want to smell smoke on your breath or clothing, and they sure don't want their hands to reek like an ashtray after you shake it. Some of the areas I've mentioned here you can do more about than others. For those you can't or won't take action on, just remember that many people will judge you, look down on you, or otherwise want to avoid you, and you'll have to work doubly hard to help them get past what you look like to find out how good you are at your job.

11. Don't fudge, even a little. There is no such thing as a "little white lie" when dealing with customers. A lie is a lie is a lie. Even when you don't outright lie but guess or ballpark and are wrong the customer—especially an SOB who's just looking for something to go wrong—believes you lied because reality at this point is irrelevant, all that matters is their perception. If you don't know, say so, find out, or explain that you don't want to say anything that could be considered confusing or misleading. It's a lot less embarrassing to not know the answer to something than to act like you do and be considered, justly or not, as a low-down liar in the end.

12. Overcome objections before they have a chance to arise. The most astute and successful salespeople I know have learned how to anticipate objections and overcome them before they ever arise. This prevents potential momentum breakers and creates a more fluid sales process.

Keep the following facts in mind concerning objections:

A. There are a handful of objections you will hear as long as you are in the selling profession. If you were selling carpets in Damascus 2,000 years ago, you heard the words, "I want to think it over," and if you're selling Mercedes on Mars 2,000 years from now, you can rest assured that you'll hear the same thing. Since these objections aren't going away you may as well learn to handle them or, better yet, to eliminate them before they surface.

B. Many of what we think of as objections are really only customer concerns. If someone asks, "what's the cheapest I can get this product," they're not objecting to the cost but merely expressing a concern. If you handle their inquiry poorly, the concern can then turn into an objection.

C. Depending on the product or service you're selling, think about the objections you hear most often and overcome them during your presentation so they don't have a chance to arise. Rather than hoping the objection doesn't come up, plant seeds in your presentation to help neutralize it. This proactive approach to selling separates the excellent salesperson from the average.

Read over the following three scenarios to see this technique in action:

Scenario One:

You are getting ready to present a product or service where you know there will be little or no discount or where you know your product sells for more than a comparable product elsewhere. You also know this may become a potential objection later when you present the price to the prospect or if he asks for a discount. It's best to gently lay the groundwork for this inevitable "there is no discount" scenario by dropping subtle clues that the customer shouldn't expect a price break. The key is to make it seem like a positive and not a negative.

At the appropriate time or place during your presentation, weave the following concept into your dialogue. Use words you are comfortable with. These are merely samples:

A. "You have great taste, Mr. Prospect. These products are so hot we have a waiting list for people who want them." Most anyone breathing the air on this planet will understand that a waiting list normally means, "You are going to be paying all the money!"

B. "The advantage of advertising on our station, Mr. Prospect, is that once you are in our rotation, you will own the hottest and most sought after spots in the entire marketplace." People expect to pay for the best and for what's hot. It feeds their ego and fills your commission check.

C. "Your timing is great, Mr. Prospect, normally we don't even have one of these products in stock and must special order them for our customers." Not only do these words help you justify a hefty price (supply and demand), but they create urgency to get it now!

D. "I can tell that quality is important to you, Mr. Prospect, because you've chosen a product/service that pays for itself over and over again in the long term. You really do get what you pay for with this product." This powerful phrase builds value, justifies the price, and assures you of very little negotiation.

My favorite definition of selling is that it is "the art of managing perceptions." If you plant seeds as indicated in the prior points and you do so early on in the sales process, your position will be more believable and credible than if you to wait to hear the "your price is too high" objection later and then have to assume a defensive posture on why you cannot discount your product.

Do not say or do things early on in the sales process that give a prospect the idea they will get a fantastic deal only to bring them tumbling back down to Earth when you show them the actual terms later. This practice *creates objections* because you have managed customers' expectation to a point where they have an unrealistic belief of what they will have to pay you, and when you show them the actual price they feel tricked, let down, or lied to. The lesson here, as strange as it sounds, is not to give your customers hope! It does you little good to get them excited about possibilities that aren't going to happen and then be forced to break the news and take the steam out of their engine. This doesn't mean that you have to scare them off with blunt, callous, "this is going to cost you" type of remarks. Just follow the finesse-based scripts in examples A through D to create the perception that they're not going to get a price break but do so in a positive, upbeat manner. This technique prevents potential SOBs and neutralizes true-blue SOBs before they have a chance to show their nasty colors.

Scenario Two:

You are preparing to present a product or service that has had quality problems in the past. Perhaps *Consumer Reports* or other media have bashed what you're selling, and you know that many customers may be aware of this reputation when they look at your product. Again, don't hold your breath and hope this concern doesn't arise by thinking you may have the one clueless prospect in the universe who didn't hear the news. Otherwise, they can use your product's reputation as a reason to slow down your efforts to close the sale, bully you into dropping the price, or shop around for something else. Again, you must plant the following seeds to manage the prospect's perception early and with great sales skill put a positive spin on things.

At the appropriate time or place, weave the following concept into your presentation. Again, these are merely samples. Use words you're comfortable with:

A. "Throughout my presentation, Mr. Prospect, I'm going to point out many of the *improvements* XYZ Brand has made in their product recently." This phrase addresses quality concerns before they have a chance to arise and force you to play defense.

B. "I'm not sure how aware you are of the many enhancements we've put into our product recently to make customers even happier and more confident than before so I want to take adequate time to point these out to you." Again, this approach puts a positive spin on where your product is and how far it has come rather than dwelling on past history.

C. "I'm not sure if you've heard about our station's market share, Mr. Prospect, but I'm pleased to report we've made steady gains over the past several reporting periods. Momentum and current trending is in our favor." This lets customers think they have a chance to hitch their product wagon to a rising star and makes less relevant any thoughts they've had that no one really listens to your station.

D. "One reason I love selling XYZ Brand, Mr. Prospect, is that they're 100% committed to improving their product. Let me share with you some of what they've done recently." This is just another way of spinning that yesterday's negative issues are history.

Again, if you address these issues before they have a chance to arise, you mostly put them to rest once and for all and can go on about your presentation knowing you've edited the prospect's confidence in what he or she is buying and minimized any concerns as well as the potential for contention to arise. The key strategy here is to preempt any resistance or negative dialogue that takes you away from setting the tone and puts you on the ropes.

It is not your duty or obligation to apologize for or confess all your product's sins of the past to a prospect. Giving too much information at this point is reckless and oftentimes irrelevant. Instead, focus on the present and the future.

Scenario Three:

Your prospect tells you right up front that he or she intends to shop the competition. Perhaps yours is the first stop they're making. They may confess that they're "just looking" and never make a decision the first time out or that they're gathering proposals from all major competitors and their committee will analyze the data and make a decision. Realize that these folks are oftentimes setting themselves up for an easier escape and planting advance seeds to take the pressure off them buying later. By acknowledging and not arguing with their initial assertion, you can take away the reason to "escape" and go elsewhere by sowing proper seeds throughout your presentation. If you do your job well here, you'll find that these prospects' need to shop elsewhere has quickly disappeared as you've given them no reason to do so.

In fact, taking away every reason the prospect may have for going elsewhere is easier than you think because, as much as people pretend to like to "wheel and deal" and shop around, most have better things to do with their time. Use the following strategies to convert a potential "wandering SOB" into a captive audience for your sales skills.

A. Do a great job of differentiating yourself from competitors with a professional and respectful approach, superior knowledge of your product, and a casual, easygoing manner.

B. Soon after the customer tells you he or she plans to shop elsewhere and isn't buying anything today, take the fight out of the process by saying something like, "I don't blame you at all for wanting to look around and make sure you're getting the best product for your money. In fact, droves of customers each year compare our product to the X, Y, and Z and still decide to buy ours. Would you like to know why?" (And then proceed into your value-building presentation.)

C. Use an evidence manual as discussed previously that compares your product or service to the competition. Present these facts to the customer so they can *see for themselves* where yours is superior. Say something like, "Mr. Prospect, since our customers' time is so important, we've tried to make their decision easier and more pleasant by doing their homework for them. May I show you how *Buyer's Guide* ranked our product against those you mentioned wanting to look at?"

What not to do:

When a prospect tells you right up front that he or she doesn't intend on buying today and wants to shop around, don't get defensive or change your tone toward the customer. Realize that this is oftentimes a defense mechanism to slow you down and you can overcome it if you employ the right techniques. Don't lose interest in the customer and get psyched out because you don't think you will make the sale today. Remember this important fact: Your customers will lie to you from time to time! I know this may not be news to some of you, but others need to stop believing everything customers say, especially things like, "I'm going to shop around and am not prepared to buy anything today." Customers can easily rationalize in their own minds the need to lie to salespeople. After all, from their standpoint, they're just trying to get the upper hand before the salesperson takes them for a ride.

13. Take the fight out of the sales process by not talking about bottom dollar price until you've had a chance to build the value in your product or service. This, of course, depends on what you're selling. Some products are far more cut and dry where price is concerned than others. When you have a product where the price is customarily negotiated or is compared rigorously to a competitor, you must buy time to establish the value in your product or service before you start playing show and tell with your bottom line figures. SOBs will oftentimes try to lure you into a bottom line price conversation long before it's wise to engage in the dialogue because until you've established value you cannot justify the price and will have to resort to defending your price to the customer in the absence of value. When you shop for something, when do you feel better about paying for it, before or after you've seen the value? When are you willing to pay more for it, before or after you've seen the value? Taking your answers into account, when do you believe it is wise to talk about the lowest possible price to a prospect, before or after he or she sees the value in what you're selling? The answer is obvious. Bypass price concerns with key phrases like those in the following scripts until you've had a chance to build the value necessary to justify the price:

Scenario: SOB customer, very early in the sales process before you've had a chance to give a presentation, asks, "How cheap can I get this one?"

"Mr. Prospect, until I've had a chance to show you what you're getting for your money, no price I mention will seem fair. After you see how our product stretches your dollars, we'll both feel better about the transaction. So let me ask you ..." And take control of the sales process back as you proceed with your investigation.

In addition to the words above, you can use the following 12 scripts depending at which stage of the sales process the SOB starts the price conversation.

Customer: "The price is too high!"

A. "Just suppose price wasn't an object, would there be anything else holding you back from wrapping this up today?" (Use this to find out if there are any other objections.)

B. "Yes, Mr. Prospect, it's not cheap. Yet thousands shop our competition each year and still come back to us to buy. Would you like to know why?" (Then get back to building value and position yourself to close the deal.)

C. "Too high as compared to what, Mr. Prospect?" (Make sure you're comparing apples to apple.)

D. "How close are we to a deal, Mr. Prospect, xxxx or yyyy?" (Then reduce to the difference to the ridiculous, as demonstrated in Chapter 3, to make the deal make sense.)

E. "Before we get too much farther along, I had better check to make sure this is still even available. Would you mind holding on while I do?" (This is called a "takeaway close." Some people don't know how badly they want something until they're about to lose it.)

F. "That's exactly why you should take it. If the price seems too high now, Mr. Prospect, the bad news is that prices on new vehicles only go up—sometimes 2–3 times per year—so the longer you wait the worse it gets. Let's lock in this price while it's as low as it is and put this shopping behind you so you can begin enjoying your new car."

G. "Yes, Mr. Prospect, but you know you get what you pay for. Did you ever get anything good that was cheap?" (Notice how with these scripts you never argue with the prospect. You reduce resistance by agreeing and then justifying your position.)

H. "Yes, Mr. Prospect, I'm sure prices are higher than the last time you looked for this product. But let me show you many of the improvement costs that are factored in to the price." (Then continue your investigation and value-building presentation.)

I. "Yes, Mr. Prospect, but I've found you can pay for the best up front or pay for the 'get by' in the end so why not start with the best?"

J. "Mr. Prospect, at ABC Decorating, price is the easy part. The tough part is picking exactly what you want out of all the different styles and arrangements. Let's focus on that first, and I promise to make you happy with the figures later." (Then proceed with your investigation and presentation.)

K. "Mr. Prospect, price is the best part, and I usually save it until after I've shown you what you're getting for your money. If that sounds fair, let me ask you ..." (Then ask an investigative question to redirect the sales process.)

L. "Mr. Prospect, I'm glad you're interested in price, but at this point I don't know your needs and wants, and any price I give you could be very misleading. Let's spend a few minutes matching you up with the service that best meets your needs, and I'll work hard to make you happy with the price later." (Then refocus on your investigation and presentation.)

Whenever transitioning from bypassing price and buying time to build value it's important to remember that whoever is asking questions is controlling the conversation. If you find yourself on the defensive and giving answer after answer, slow the SOB down by asking him a question concerning the purchase:

"Mr. Prospect, I forgot to ask, are you going to be using this product primarily for business or for personal use?" Then ask another question and another until you're on the right track with the investigative and rapport-building process and back in control of the transaction.

One very successful salesperson I know takes the fight out of the sales process by posting a sign on his office wall with the Oscar Wilde quote: "A cynic is one who knows the price of everything and the value of nothing." In a subtle, tongue-in-check manner, this technique discourages customers from making price the primary issue during the purchase. If it fits your style, you may consider including the same practice in your own sales arsenal to take the wind out of SOBs before they have a chance to get gusty.

SOB Summary for Chapter 4: Take the Fight Out of the Sales Process!

Do everything in your power to avoid annoying, irritating, antagonizing, or offending customers with the wrong words, tone, attitude, or appearance. This will stop normal prospects from be-

coming obnoxious or belligerent and tame those who are naturally in that state.

1. Look and sound like you really want to be at work. You
   will attract into your life what you project with your
   own attitude. If you think the world is a cesspool, you'll
   only notice and draw to you the vermin.

2. Avoid too much hype in your presentations. It makes
   you sound disingenuous, unprofessional, and just plain
   full of it. You will also create expectations difficult to live
   up to.

3. Don't knock the competition. This makes you look
   small, mean, immature, and sarcastic.

4. Don't talk down to anyone in the buying party. Respect
   is reciprocal and so is condescension.

5. Don't sprinkle your presentation with profanity or off-
   color stories. You are in a serious profession, act like it.

6. Don't begin the investigative process too soon. They've
   got to buy into you before they buy into what you're
   selling so take the time to establish common ground.

7. Don't argue with a customer, even if you're right. It is
   exhausting, expensive, and just plain foolish to start or
   jump into fights you cannot possibly win.

8. Avoid the words, "that's not my job." Say that often
   enough and you'll be able to recite a new line, "I'm
   looking for a job."

9. Plant seeds to lower the customer's expectations. Don't
   create false hope. Bring prospects down to reality gently.
   You cannot antagonize people and expect to sell them
   at the same time.

10. Know that customers will judge you. Do all you can to
    look and sound like a pro at all times. Character, com-

petence, and sincerity help prospects get past how you look or sound, but don't expect them all to warm up to you right away. Some never will. What you "are" may scream so loudly at them that they can't even hear what you say.

11. Don't fudge, even a little. If you tell a little white lie, you're still a liar. The truth may hurt for a moment, but lying to a customer can kill your career.

12. Overcome objections before they have a chance to come up. Initiate a preemptive strike against the objections you hear most often. Taking the offensive stops you from playing defense when a customer brings them up later.

13. Buy time to build value before you get duped into talking bottom dollar price. If the prospect doesn't see the value, no price will seem fair anyhow.

5 | How to Face and Finesse the SOB "Quadruple Threat"!

Let's Start with Straight Talk

There are numerous threats that inhibit you from selling stubborn, obnoxious, and belligerent customers. This chapter will cover four of them: customers who delight in telling you they're shopping your competitor; inconsiderate louts who make appointments and then never show up; "third-basemen"—the helpful know-it-alls a prospect brings with him to give him advice and stop you from ripping him off, and the delusional customer who has price expectations so unrealistic that you're convinced the drugs he did in high school have resulted in his room temperature I.Q. With the right skills and finesse, you can succeed in these situations and spend your vacations at the Ritz while your competitors eat sloppy joes at the Super 8.

1. Overcoming Threat #1: Sell effectively against the competition. There is a logical sequence you should follow when customers point out that they are comparing your product or service to a competitor's. Many salespeople get nervous or overanxious at this point and begin saying too much, resort to negativity or sarcasm, or become confrontational. Here is a trio of sequential steps to follow that will professionally, quickly, and convincingly help you sell against competitors.

> **A. Identify the customer's buying motives or hot buttons.** Before unloading too much information about your product and how it compares, slow down and get specific. Determine exactly what the customer's buying motives are. What are his or her hot buttons? When it comes time to compare your product to the competition, you want the differences to resonate with the prospect and to be highly relevant. The only way you can accomplish this is if you are comparing the features or benefits of the products that mean the most to the customer.

> **B. Present your product as it specifically compares to those hot buttons.** Reframe your presentation to present selectively the areas of the customer's greatest interest where your product or service has the advantage. How your product compares to another in areas outside the customer's primary interest—his or her buying motives—will be irrelevant to the prospect and may be

perceived as a diversionary trick to shift the focus away from what is most important to the buyer. Compare hot buttons to hot buttons and you'll gather more momentum in your presentation, captivate the SOBs interest, and move closer to the sale. Ramble on about a plethora of trivial differences that the customer could not care less about and you make him less likely to want to buy from you since you are talking too much and wasting his time. This makes the prospect more likely to go and take a closer look at what the competition has to offer.

C. If the SOB gets hung up on picking apart one or two minor items as a reason not to buy, use an appropriate response, similar to the following scripts, as a strategy to put matters in perspective.

"Mr. Prospect, is your decision to invest in a new vehicle going to be based on one cubic foot of trunk space or on the many safety and convenience features you told me were so important to you and your family?"

"Mr. Prospect, when it comes right down to making your final decision, which factor will be most important to you: saving three cents per gallon or having a higher quality and longer lasting additive for your customers that will keep them coming back for more?"

If the prospect answers that "they're both important," put things in greater perspective by replying with,

"I understand, but which is *most* important?"

"The main thing is to keep the main thing the main thing." —Stephen Covey

---

As you can imagine, in order to utilize this strategy for successfully selling against your competition, you will need an in-depth knowledge of your own product's attributes as well as what your competitor offers. If your product doesn't score well when comparing the areas that your customer stated were most important to him, try to expand his buying motives into areas where you know yours has an edge. For instance, if their primary interest is safety and the competitive product they're looking at has an edge in this area but you know that your product is rated higher in dependability and economy, shift the focus of the conversation and broaden their buying motives by asking,

"I'm happy to hear you say that safety means a lot to you because our product compares quite well in that area. In addition to safety, would you also say that dependability and economy are going to be important to you?" (Can you imagine anyone answering "no" to this question?)

The customer most probably will answer in the affirmative; when she does, start your presentation with the areas where your product does have an advantage in safety (and avoid those where it doesn't) and then proceed to spend more time presenting the dependability and economical advantages your product has.

2. Overcoming Threat #2: Make sure prospects show up for their appointments. Sometimes customers can be downright thoughtless, unprofessional, and inconsiderate. They agree to come in on a certain day and at a specific time and then they don't show up, and in many cases they don't even call to let you know about it. This displays a vast disrespect for your time. It may also evince that the customer is just plain forgetful, selfish, or otherwise clueless. Regardless of the reason for their failure to keep their word, it wastes your day, breaks your momentum, and can be demoralizing. Many times salespeople are to fault for customers failing to show. They don't have the skills to set credible appointments or neglect to create the perception that they are a professional and that their time is valuable. As salespeople, we also tend to give prospects too much benefit of the doubt, assume they'll do what they say, and mistakenly believe that once we set the appointment our job is done, when in fact it is just beginning. By following the next few steps you can drastically increase the chances that a customer actually shows up for an appointment or will at least call and reschedule if they can't make it.

Setting appointments that stick:

A. After you and a prospect agree on the time for an appointment, your job is not over; it's just beginning. Too many salespeople so rejoice when they set an appointment that they fail to spend 60 more seconds planting the seeds that virtually guarantee a prospect will show up or call if he or she can't. Think of setting the appointment as a starting gate and not a finish line.

B. Once you set the appointment, anchor the appointment with commitment. Anchoring appointments creates a stronger commitment from the customer to show up or at least to call if they cannot make it. When you anchor your appointment you create a perception that the appointment is serious, and that your time is worth something and generate a mental picture that obligates the customer to show up or call if he or she cannot.

Following is a sample script that you use immediately after you've agreed on the appointment time. This script is assuming you are setting the appointment over the telephone, but you can use the same principles when anchoring an appointment with a person in your presence.

Mr. Jones, please grab a pen and paper. I have something I'd like you to write down. (With this line, you assume control of the conversation.) *My name is Dave Anderson and my phone number is 650-941-1493.* (This increases the odds that customers will remember your name and gives them your number so they can call if something comes up.) *If you'll also write down our appointment time of 2:40 on the 12th, I'm going to write it down on my calendar as well.* (This further commits them to show up and builds credibility that you're taking the appointment seriously and expect them do to the same.) *What I'll do is take myself off the sales floor before you arrive and have a Suburban cleaned up and pulled to the side for you to look at. Do you drink coffee or something cold?*

. . . Great, I'll have a fresh pot brewed for you and waiting. If something comes up with my schedule to interfere with our appointment, I'll call you right away so we can reschedule. Could you please do the same for me? I look forward seeing you at 2:40 on Tuesday. (You've just painted a mental picture of setting special time aside for the customer. He or she now visualizes you taking yourself off the sales floor, cleaning up the vehicle, and brewing coffee. This will further obligate them to show up or to at least call if they cannot.)

I used vehicle sales in this example, but you can tweak the script to fit whatever you sell. Please notice that I also used an odd time with which to set the appointment: 2:40. This makes it memorable, and because it seems more precise it will further create the perception that your time is valuable and you expect them to do what they say and either show up or call to let you know they're not coming.

C. Managers should confirm the call. Whenever possible, the appointment should be confirmed at least one day before the actual appointment. And it is better if someone else calls to confirm the appointment, preferably someone with a title that sounds like they have authority (manager, customer service coordinator, etc.). If this isn't feasible for you, then you can confirm them yourself and still have a very positive effect. The great thing about the script I'm going to share with you is that even if you cannot reach the person by telephone, it is appropriate to leave as a message and still have a high impact.

"Mr. Prospect, my name is Dave Anderson, and I'm the sales manager at We Will Rock You Music Store. I noticed that you have an appointment at 3:10 tomorrow with Jack Black to look at our new Fender guitar line. I wanted to call and thank you in advance for coming in and give you the number to my direct line in case something comes up and you can't reach Jack. It is 818-905-1123. I hope I have a chance to meet you tomorrow and want to thank you again for taking the time to visit us."

When I was responsible for the sales operations of automotive dealerships, each store that reported to me had a daily appointment quota and sales managers were required to call and confirm the appointments. At the end of each day I received an appointment reconciliation sheet that showed how many appointments were set for the day, how many customers actually showed up, how many of them we sold, and how many appointments were confirmed for the following day. There was also a line where the manager confirming the appointment would write his or her initials. Without fail, the appointments confirmed by a manager were three times as likely to show up as those that were not.

3. Overcoming Threat #3: Dealing successfully with "third basemen." A "third baseman" is another person a buyer brings along to offer advice and expertise in making a purchase. Oftentimes, first-time buyers bring a third baseman to help stop them from making a mistake. Third basemen are also known as "experts," "know-it-alls," and general pains in the rear end. However, with the right attitude, finesse, and skill you can turn a third baseman into an ally who will help you make the sale.

Some background on third basemen:

A third baseman is someone the buyer obviously trusts and respects so becoming adversarial will assure that you immediately build a wall between you and the sale. The prospect's relationship with a third baseman is much more important than his or her relationship with you or the product or service you're selling. Thus, even if they really want what you're selling, they will feel obligated to get it somewhere else if you insult, offend, or alienate the third baseman in any way. From the third basemen's standpoint, they feel they must do or say something to justify the fact they have come along to help with the purchase. Bearing this in mind, you can follow the outlined steps to create a more positive and profitable experience the next time a customer brings Mr. or Mrs. Helper with them to work you over.

A. Acknowledge the third baseman and his or her role and expertise. Say something like, "It's great to meet you. I wish I would have had someone to help me with my first car purchase," or "when I bought my first house," etc. This takes any potential fight out of the process early on.

B. Use collaborative phrases that lay down positive ground rules and set the tone for a non-confrontational sales transaction. These are similar to those I presented in Chapter 4.

"Folks, throughout the process, if I'm going too fast, just let me know. If you have questions, please ask them. If I don't know the answer, I can find out, and if I'm showing you something you don't like, let me know and we'll move on. If we all work together, I can promise you that you'll leave here with the right product and a great deal."

C. Never, ever let your ego get in the way of the sales process because a third baseman aggravates or frustrates you. Keep the big picture in mind. Remember the words of Zig Ziglar, "You can feed your ego or you can feed your family."

D. Include the third baseman in your presentation. Don't forget that your primary attention should be given to the buyer, but include the third baseman in your conversation by making eye contact and giving him the chance to ask questions.

E. Never, ever, embarrass the third baseman by demeaning or belittling a question or concern. This can turn both the primary buyer and the third baseman into SOBs. Navigate your encounter with a third baseman using skill and diplomacy. You'll know you've done your job well when, while trying to close the sale, the third baseman turns to the buyer and says, "You need to take this deal."

4. Overcoming Threat #4: Pie-in-the-sky expectations. Customers often have an unrealistic set of expectations concerning the cost for your product or service. Normally, this is because they haven't done their homework and are ignorant. This type of customer is to be expected and is fairly easy to deal with once you can educate them as to the reality of, and build enough value to justify, the price. What is less forgivable is the unskilled, thoughtless, blabber mouth salesperson who stupidly creates a set of expectations so high that he can never live up to it later. This leaves the customer feeling disillusioned, let down, betrayed, and even deceived. After years of working in the automotive retail business I've seen too often how a salesperson would get a customer's hopes up about the amount of money he'd get for his trade-in only to look like a fool later when he had to show the buyer the actual trade value, making the customer one angry SOB. At the same time, I've seen far too many sales amateurs raise the hopes of a prospect for what he or she might be able to buy a vehicle for only to create the same level of disappointment when it came time to show the real numbers. For a profession of people dependent on repeat and referral business in order to secure a six-figure income, the practice of creating an artificially high set of expectations is self-destructive. While I pick on the automotive industry in this example, far too many industries partake in their own version of this madness through misleading advertising and untrained sales teams. Look over the following scenarios I've seen firsthand more times than I care to recall and learn the principles these examples support:

Sabotage Scenario One:

A prospect comes in and shows an interest in an over-aged vehicle (one that has been on the lot a long, long time and needs to go) that the manager is extremely motivated to sell. Without meaning any harm, a foolish salesperson says something like, "I'll tell you one thing. My boss would make you a once-in-a-lifetime deal on this one. This car is on our 'hit list' and has got to go."

When prospects are standing there in front of you and you have control of the sales process, why say something to raise their expectations so high the only possible outcome is to let them down when you actually show them the figures? Even if you do offer them an incredible deal, most customers won't appreciate the reality of what you're proposing. This is because the perception you created with your "once-in-a-lifetime" offer made them think you'd nearly give them the product for free. Remember, there is no reality, there is only perception, and selling is the art of managing those perceptions.

Can you really blame a customer for turning into an SOB after he's invested his valuable time with you during the sales process under the impression that he's getting the deal of a lifetime only to find out his perceptions have been horribly mismanaged by a careless salesperson?

Sabotage Scenario Two:

A prospect asks you what you think his or her trade-in (car, boat, RV, motorcycle, piece of jewelry, office machinery, or the many other products now commonly accepted as trade-ins on new products) is worth and you respond with, "I'm not sure, but I can tell you my manager is going to love your XXX. It's one of the cleanest, nicest XXX I've seen in quite some time."

Since most people believe what they're trading in is worth far more than it is, you just aided and abetted their disillusionment with the hope-inducing hype like the phrase above. When you say something like this, you raise their expectations to a level you won't be able to meet later, and you have no one to blame for losing the deal but yourself. No one did you in, you opened your mouth and stupid sounds fell out as you stuffed your foot right in it.

Even if someone tries to bait you into admitting what a nice product their trade-in is, stay professionally neutral. Just reply with, "Yes Mr. Customer, it is a nice boat. In fact, we've been really lucky recently because we've had a bunch of very nice boats come in on trade." In a polite way you're telling the prospect that his "nice trade-in" is nothing special, even as you acknowledge that it is indeed nice.

The moral of these two examples and similar situations is never give your customers too much hope where financial expectations are concerned. Once you raise their thinking to an irrationally exuberant level, there's only one way the thinking can go from there: down. And your chances of making the sale go right down with it since the emotional reaction they're likely to have once they feel tricked or deceived will seal your fate.

SOB Summary for Chapter 5: How to Face and Finesse the SOB "Quadruple Threat"!

1. Sell effectively against the competition by narrowing your focus to the buying motives the prospect holds most dear. Then compare your product/service in those areas and show how yours delivers a clear advantage.

2. If your product doesn't deliver a clear advantage in the arenas of their prime buying motives, reframe the presentation by expanding their hot buttons to those more favorable to your product.

3. Make sure appointments actually show up by anchoring your appointments with commitments and having someone with an authoritative title confirm the appointment.

4. Deal effectively with third basemen by taking the potential awkwardness out by saying, "I think it's great you came along. I wish I had someone to help me when I bought my XXXX."

5. Remember that the buyer's first loyalty is to the third baseman and that they will walk away from whatever you're selling—even if they love it—if they feel that buying it will harm the relationship they have with their third baseman. Because of this you should never belittle, ignore, talk down to, or embarrass a third baseman.

6. Diminish the unrealistic expectations an ignorant customer has by taking the time to educate them and build value in what you're selling. But never create a false set of expectations with careless words, hyped-up claims, or promises. Your customers will take their resentment and sense of betrayal and go elsewhere.

6

Shovel the Piles While They're Small!

Let's Start with Straight Talk

Some customers seem to have a degree in disagreement. If you didn't know better you'd think they were deliberately trying to provoke you, mess with your head, or get something for nothing. Other customers don't start out to make life difficult. They have a problem or concern that doesn't get handled to their satisfaction and it brings out their worst. Indifferent and unskilled salespeople fan their flames of discontent with a combination of short, snappy answers; passive aggressive body language; a crummy attitude; or a terse tone. While the first step to making sure a customer's smoldering ember doesn't turn into a raging inferno is to engage in a bit of fire prevention by following many of the strategies in this book, you also need tactics to slow down, disarm, or neutralize the natural born bully. In both cases, it's best to shovel the piles while they're small. In other words, correct the problem in its early stages so that a molehill of trouble doesn't turn into Mt. Everest.

Learning What Not to Do from Davis

I once worked with a salty, weather-beaten, chain-smoking, alcoholic car salesman named Davis who had a knack of escalating the tension when a customer copped an attitude toward him. Once, when a prospect at our dealership refused several times to give his name, Davis replied between puffs of his Marlboro, "Well, I've got to call you something. I guess I'll call you Mr. Prick. Come right this way, Mr. Prick, and we'll see if we can find a car with a seat that will work loose whatever it is you've got stuck up your backside." Needless to say, the customer stormed off leaving a cloud of profanity in his wake. Davis laughed for weeks about how he "told off Mr. Prick," but he lost sight of something in the process: He failed to make the sale, he didn't get a referral, and "Mr. Prick" bought from a competitor. The moral of the story is that not everyone you're going to have the opportunity to sell will be a barrel of fun. Some will be rude. Others will look down on you. Others still will provoke you. Many will be moochers who exaggerate their dissatisfaction in hopes of getting something for free. The best revenge you can dish out to these folks is to sell them and take their money while you maintain your own self-respect and keep your character intact throughout the process. It's not always easy. But it is bankable.

Six Strategies for Dealing with Ticked-Off Customers

1. Always begin your answer to the customer's problem with the words, "I'm sorry." "I'm sorry" helps take the fight out of the situation and can disarm the customer.

Customers are very apprehensive when they first bring a problem to someone's attention and oftentimes expect the worst. A humble response settles SOBs down and gives them a sense of relief. How many times have you heard someone say, "All I really wanted was an apology" or "He never even said he was sorry."

2. Get angry *with* but never *at* the customer. If you get angry at the same things that make your customers angry, it's nearly impossible for customers to be angry with you! Say something like:

"I hate it when that happens," or "That should never have happened," or "That would make me so mad. In light of what has happened, you're handling things very well."

3. Ask the customer what it will take to make things right. In many cases customers will ask for less than you would have offered. Most of the time they are so happy to see you taking responsibility they don't ask for much of anything. However, the longer it takes to solve the issue and the more irritated customers become the higher their price to fix it. Before you worry too much about what it will cost to keep your current customer happy and coming back to do business in the future, you should consider that the Technical Assistance Research Programs (TARP) estimates that it costs 5.7 times more to get a new customer than to retain a devoted one.[1]

4. Take them to your leader. Why? Because the boss often can say yes when you have to say no. If they are asking for something you are unauthorized to approve, don't hassle them, just take them to the boss. SOBs often will ask to speak to the boss anyhow, so in this manner you preempt their need to do so. Rather than catch your boss by surprise by dropping by his office with a ticked off SOB, make sure you clue him in first and privately on what is happening.

5. Never pass the buck. You should own whatever problem a customer brings to you. Never suggest they ask for someone else. If necessary take them to the other person. Even if you can't solve the issue you still own the issue until someone else takes ownership. The last thing someone with a problem wants is more hoops to jump through that exacerbate his or her aggravation.

6. Avoid antagonistic phrases. Whatever words you choose to say and how you choose to say them will quickly elevate or deflate the problem. Thus, you cannot afford to be casual or careless in your response. Stay away from dumb stuff like:

> A. "That's not my job." This incendiary phrase is just looking for trouble. Instead say,
>   "I'm sorry you're having a problem with that. Let's go find the person who can help us solve it."
>   Or,
>   "I am really sorry you're having to spend your time on something like this. Let's see about getting it fixed right now."
> B. "You'll have to speak to Mr. Jones." First, this is passing the buck. Second, people don't like to be told what they'll have to do—especially when they're already upset. Say instead,
>   "I'm sorry you're having trouble with this, let me help you find Mr. Jones so he can tell us how to solve it."

By re-reading these six points you should quickly discern that the most effective method for handling angry customers begins with immediately lowering tension—shoveling the piles while they're small—and taking the fight out of the process rather than escalating matters with the wrong words, tone, or attitude. The first few seconds of the encounter are the key. They will set the tone for the rest of the transaction and have a great bearing on whether the customer becomes your worst enemy or an unwavering advocate.

Learning from Marriott

The Marriott Hotel chain surveyed tens of thousands of guests who had stayed at their hotels in an effort to find out how likely they were to return to a Marriott. Those surveyed fell into three categories: customers with no problems at all during their stay, those who had an unresolved problem during their stay, and guests with a resolved problem during their stay.[2]

Here's what it found:

1. 89% of the guests with no problem at all said they would return to a Marriott. Obviously, not everyone was impressed, but wouldn't we all like to retain 89% of our customers?

2. 69% of guests with an unresolved problem said they'd return to a Marriott. Many people are unforgiving. You have one chance to get it right and that's it. Percentage-wise, Marriott lost a significant portion of their customers by failing to resolve a customer problem to their satisfaction.

3. 94% of guests who had a problem that was resolved declared they would return to a Marriott. Read it again. Nearly all of them would come back despite having a temporary setback during their stay. This valuable survey teaches us one great lesson: Customers who have a problem that is handled well are more loyal than customers with no problem at all.

Anyone can make a mistake and drop the ball from time to time. That's not the point. Rather, the main thing is how will you handle this when it happens? Shovel the piles while they're small! And remember that it's not just what you say but how you say it when dealing with customers. Too many of us put a smile on our face but betray our actual feelings with an annoyed, indifferent, or sarcastic tone.

What to Do When You Make a Mistake

To err is human. The problem is that when you are in sales prospects oftentimes assume the worst: you intentionally misled them, lied by omission, or were just plain incompetent. Living in an age when people seem less and less willing to take responsibility for their mistakes, or for their lives in general, you can minimize the damage you do and stand above the crowd of victim-driven whiners when you screw up by doing the following:

1. Admit your mistake and take responsibility for it. If the mistake was your fault, say so. If you gave the wrong information, admit it. Don't blame or use excuses like, "I was having a bad day," etc. Just say, "I have no excuse. I made a mistake, and this is what it is." You'll be surprised how well that goes over and how refreshing it is in times like these when the multitudes delight in absolving themselves from responsibility by living in a gray area with no absolutes: no right and wrong, no success or failure, and no good or bad.

2. Do whatever is in your power to make things right. Being responsible is more than just making confessions. It is also taking action to right the wrong.

3. If the prospect remains unforgiving, reiterate your apology without getting defensive. Say something like the following and say it sincerely, "I truly apologize that this happened to you. Sometimes it just stinks to be a fallible human being." Even the toughest SOB will have a hard time kicking you when you're down after admitting you're the same thing that he or she is: a fallible human being.

"When you make a mistake there are three things you should do: admit it, learn from it and don't repeat it." —Coach Paul "Bear" Bryant

---

Shoveling the Piles While They're Small Is Good Economics

For the many supervisors reading this passage, I would expect you've found that by the time a customer problem reaches your desk it costs you much more to make the customer happy than if it had been handled at a lower level. And I'm not only talking about the extra dollars but the valuable man-hours wasted as the issue lingers. You can then add the cost of the unhappy customer telling more and more people each day how poorly he's being treated by your organization as he seeks to get an issue resolved. This is why it is good economics to train and empower your people to handle customer problems at the lowest possible levels without having to check with two supervisors and obtain multiple signatures.

Putting on the Ritz

While staying at the Ritz Carlton in Battery Park right across from the Statue of Liberty, I had an excellent customer experience with two exceptions: Both days that I turned my laundry in to be dry cleaned it was never brought back to my room. I had to get on the phone two nights in a row and ask them to track it down. It wasn't a really big deal, but it is still a bit inconvenient when you're traveling, preparing to give a series of speeches, and have more important details with which to deal. Upon checking out, the clerk asked me if everything during my stay was satisfactory, and I told her that everything was great but that I thought they might have a communication breakdown between the laundry and bell staff since the clothes (there were several suits and shirts) weren't returned to my room in two consecutive nights. Without missing a beat, the clerk pulled up my account on her computer and said, "Mr. Anderson, I'm sorry you had that problem. I've removed the charges (it was around $200.00) from your bill." I was stunned and protested that I didn't expect anything for free, that the quality of the cleaning was fine, but that I thought she should know about the issue. She wouldn't hear of my protests, and the charges stayed off the bill. Notably, she didn't have to check with a supervisor, phone anyone for approval, or consult a "customer relations" handbook to decide what to do. I can't even count how many times I've repeated this story or estimate how many thousands of people have heard it in my speeches or how many hundreds of thousands will read it here. But do keep this in mind: Studies show that unhappy customers tell far more people about their problems than happy customers. It is estimated that one unhappy customer tells at least 10 others and that 13 percent of unhappy customers become "corporate terrorists" telling at least 20 other people just to get even with you.[3] Thus, if you're in the habit of ticking people off, ripping them off, or putting them off, before long you'll be able to fill an entire football stadium with people who avoid your business at all costs.

Last-Resort Responses to Card-Carrying SOBs

Let's say you have a genuine SOB on the phone who is irate with you or your company. He is abusive, profane, and is possibly even threatening you. Talk to enough customers and this scenario is going to happen from time to time. The problem is that if you don't have a plan, you're likely to react poorly and escalate the tension rather than defuse it. Follow the two strategies outlined by my friend Zig Ziglar on how to properly handle these potentially explosive situations and retain your customers at the same time[4]:

Strategy One: Go Silent. Say nothing.

Absolute silence will surprise and, more important, calm the angry person. Cursers are often "provokers" who are looking for a word fight. Why play their game? Pause until the person asks, "Are you still there?" At that point, if you want to have a little fun and "win the client over" instead of "winning over the client," pick out a portion of the tirade that was the most ridiculous and exaggerated. Say, "As I understand it, your major problem is _____." And then you repeat in a clear, concise manner what was just said. The odds are good that the client, with some embarrassment, will confess that maybe things weren't quite that bad.

Strategy Two: Professionally, but firmly draw the line:

"Mr. Prospect, when you talk to me like that, I feel I can no longer be helpful to you. If you will work with me and focus on the problem, I believe we can come up with a solution. However, if you continue to use profane and abusive language, my integrity demands that I terminate this conversation."

If the abuse continues, do as you have promised. If you are dealing with someone on the phone, allow for a "cooling off" time and then call back. Chances are excellent that he will be embarrassed by his behavior and will be much easier to work with. At this point you are in an excellent position to solve the problem or make the sale. Here's why: The prospect or customer feels that he did something *to* you and now he should do something *for* you. That something could include an apology, a willingness to listen, and even a desire to "make it right" by buying or continuing to buy from you.

Life is too short to allow yourself to become a punching bag for SOBs who cross the line and verbally abuse you. But at the same time, it's vital to your long-term business interests that you should be more interested in winning the person than in winning the argument. As Abraham Lincoln once said, "The best way I know to defeat an enemy is to make him my friend."

SOB Summary for Chapter 6: Shovel the Piles While They're Small!

1. The first words you should use when addressing a dissatisfied customer are, "I'm sorry."

2. Get angry *with* but never *at* the customer.

3. Ask the customer what it will take to make things right.

4. Take them to your leader.

5. Never pass the buck.

6. Avoid antagonistic phrases or tones or a defensive attitude.

7. Remember that customers with a problem that you solve quickly are more loyal than customers with no problems at all.

8. Shovel the piles while they're small by solving customer issues at the lowest possible levels in your organization. This is good business economics because the longer a customer problem persists and the higher it goes up the ladder for resolution the more expensive it is.

9. When you make a mistake admit it, offer to make it right, and don't get defensive if the SOB has a hard time

forgiving you. Your calm and humble manner will wear them down and win them over.

10. Let the fact that unhappy customers tell far more people about their experience than the happy ones motivate you to shovel the piles while they're small.

7 | Create a Cult!

Let's Start with Straight Talk

It's embarrassing to be in a sales position for years or decades and have to race new salespeople out to catch a customer because you never took care of the people you sold all those years; you didn't follow up after the sale; you did nothing to make them remember you; you took them for granted, and now they have no reason to ever come back to see you or to refer others to you. I worked with a guy like this at in my first car dealership job as a salesman. Jay had been at the dealership for nearly 30 years, and what I remember about him is that, after three decades of working in the same place, he still had to race the brand new salespeople out to catch a customer in the 110-degree Texas heat because he did nothing to build a relationship with the customers he sold in nearly half a lifetime. At the end of the month his sales numbers were average or below. What does this have to do with selling SOBs? Everything! Repeat and referral customers are always easier to sell than fresh customers who don't know you, like you, or trust you yet. They also give higher customer satisfaction scores and send droves of referrals your way over the years.

The best way to deal with fewer SOBs is to learn to retain the customers you already have and gain referrals from them. In fact, a worthy goal of anyone in sales should be to become *less* dependent on fresh customers each year that goes by. This doesn't mean you shun new business or fail to seek it out, it means instead that you rely less on it to make a living, and many of the new accounts you do acquire serve as "gravy" that shoots your income into the six-figure range. The most successful salespeople I've met in any field have created a cult of loyal followers who wouldn't think of buying elsewhere. You can do the same. Even if you're like Jay and have been in the business for decades and have never built the type of following that has provided you financial security, you can begin right away. As the old saying goes, "While you cannot go back and start over my friend, you can start today and make a new end."

Lessons from the World's Greatest Salesman

The *Guiness Book of World Records* listed car salesman, Joe Girard, as the world's greatest salesman 12 times! And while Joe sold cars, you can learn from his lessons and apply them to whatever you sell. First, here's some background on Joe: He sold 267 cars his first year in the car business (the average car salesperson today sells between eight and 10 units per month). By his fourth year he was up to 614 car and truck retail sales. After just a few years in the business, 60% of his customers were repeat buyers and the other 40% were referrals.[1] The last several years of his career he averaged selling five cars per day. Joe's secrets to success are as valid today as when he was setting world records.

Following are four of Joe's best tips for creating a cult:

1. **Don't join the club.**
   "I did learn one important lesson very early in my career. <u>Don't join the club.</u> Most salespeople learn it their first

day in a new place but soon forget it. What it means is this: Don't become a part of what we call the "dope ring" or the "bull ring" in the place where you work. That is where all the guys get together in the morning and spend their time discussing what they did last night, or what their wife was complaining about at breakfast or some other subject that has nothing to do with work." Joe Girard[2]

Thoughts on not joining the club:

A. The more unmanaged time you leave in your schedule the more time you are likely to spend in the "club." Unmanaged time flows to your weaknesses and to the trivial. Schedule your priorities and structure your day the night before you come to work. Then work your daily plan with intensity.

B. Think about the people you hang around with at work most often: Do they move you closer to or farther away from your goals? The next time you find yourself huddled up gossiping, reminiscing, or complaining with the "Fellowship of the Miserable" ask yourself, "How much money is this making me right now, will I be able to someday take what I'm doing at this very moment and cash it at the bank?" Trade in the time you're spending in the club for time spent following up working deals, on the phone with or sending regular mailers to your current customer base, building lifelong relationships, differentiating yourself from the one-month sales wonders polluting the selling profession, and making yourself less dependent on new customers.

C. If you're in the "club," work your way out of it right away. You don't have to make enemies of or isolate members of the "club" when you decide to leave it. Just start spending more time on being productive and they'll soon realize you're not as "fun" as you used to be and let you do your own thing. "I have stayed in the same place all these years because what counts most is *how* you work not *where* you work. We have a good location like everyone else and our pay plan is about the same as well. So I have found out that what counts most is how *smart* I work, which is even more important than how *hard* I work." Joe Girard[3]

2. Understand Girard's Law of 250. Every time you turn off just one prospect, your turn off 250 more!

"At Catholic funeral homes, they give out mass cards with name and picture of the departed. I asked an undertaker how he determined the number of cards to print up, and he told me that experience over the years showed the average number of people that came to funerals was 250. A short time later I asked a Protestant funeral director who bought a car from me how many people came to see a body or attend a funeral, and he told me 250. Then one day at a wedding I asked the man who ran the catering the average number of guests at a wedding, and he told me, 'about 250 from the bride's and 250 from the groom's.' I guess you can figure out what Girard's Law of 250 is, but I'll tell you anyway: Everyone knows 250 people in his or her life important enough to be invited to a wedding and to the funeral!" Joe Girard[4]

Based on Girard's Law of 250, if you upset only two people per month, by the end of the year there could be 6,000 people negatively influenced by those disgruntled customers. To take this a step further, if you stay in the business for 15 years or so, you could have the equivalent of a good-sized town filled with people who would choose to avoid you, if given the opportunity to do so.

3. Treat your customers better than anyone else. If you strictly see dollar signs when you look at a customer it will come through in your words and actions. But if you see the potential to establish a lifelong, mutually beneficial relationship that attitude will come through as well. The good news is that customers have become so accustomed to indifference, apathy, and outright rudeness when dealing with salespeople that it doesn't take much to stand out from the pack.

Not long ago, my wife bought a new car from a dealership just a few miles from our house in Southern California. I was out of town at the time but returned in time to go with her to sign the paperwork and take delivery. The salesman rushed us through how the features worked and, to this day, we're still not sure what some of the buttons are for. However, he made a point of taking out a copy of the customer satisfaction survey and admonishing us that he needed to get a perfect score. We've yet to receive a follow-up call, a thank-you note, or any type of mailer/newsletter from the salesperson or the Mercedes dealership where she made the purchase. Amateurs like this pretender are why I tell salespeople in my seminars that their number one opportunity in sales is the very high number of average and below average salespeople who lose more sales than they ever make, who stand out only because they were pathetic rather than professional, and who treat our great profession more like a garbage dump than the goldmine it really is. It is true that the swelling ranks of short-sighted morons walking around with "sales consultant" on their name badge ought to make professional salespeople bound out of bed in the morning and skip all the way to work.

4. Send mailers that actually get read. Contact *after* the sale is what establishes a strong customer relationship and helps guarantee you repeat and referral purchases from the just-sold customer. But it does little good to send follow-up notes, letters, and the like if they don't get read.

Fool your mailing list. "I send 12 pieces of mail to my mailing list every year and each piece is a different shape and color envelope. I never put the name of my business on the outside of the envelope. In January you will get a message that says: HAPPY NEW YEAR! I LIKE YOU! It has a nice piece of artwork on it, appropriate to the season and is signed, 'Joe Girard, Merollis Chevrolet. That is all the sell you get.'" Joe Girard[5]

When is the last time you received a thank-you note from the person who sold you furniture, your computer, jewelry, advertising for your business, or your house?

5. Build a pipeline of future prospects. Don't wait until you have a bad month to get serious about prospecting. It should be a regular discipline. Remember, you're building your future business and choosing which group of customers you would rather work with over time: friends and repeat and referral customers. "If you've ever seen a Ferris Wheel you know how it works. One at a time, the guy in charge fills the seats. People get off, he fills their seats, moves the wheel a little, fills the next seats, and so on until all the people in the seats have left and new ones come on. Good selling is like that too. Only the wheel is always moving just a little bit so that some people—the ones you have just sold—can get off for a while and others—the ones you are just starting to work on—can get on." Joe Girard[6]

Three strategies for building a pipeline of future prospects:

A. Ask for referrals from everyone whom you just sold. Make this a day-in, day-out discipline. If you fail to ask, it's not simple forgetfulness. It's a sign of complacency. You should ask right after you've made the sale. Chances are good that the customer will never be happier with you than she is right now so seize the moment. Until you've tried to turn one deal into two or three, you haven't truly maximized your customer, regardless of how much money you made on the deal.

B. Maintain ongoing contact with your sold customer base. Never take the people you sold for granted. In addition to being just plain dumb it is sales suicide. Depending on the size of your customer base, they should hear from you by phone at least two or three times per year as you follow up and get a monthly or quarterly newsletter from you. Keep the newsletter simple: one page. In it you can include everything from a quote of the month to a favorite recipe to specials you're running at your business to maintenance tips for the product they bought and so forth. What's even better is if you can email them this newsletter and save the printing and postage costs. Even if they rarely read the actual content of what you send them, you'll be making a consistent marketing impression on them and they'll think of you first the next time they buy or refer a friend. You will also stand out as a professional in a crowded field of sales wannabes.

Have you ever had your realtor, furniture salesperson, car salesman, banker, sales representative to your business, or your jeweler send you this type of correspondence consistently? If so, I bet you can quickly recite their name and would be likely to call them again the next time you need a service they provide. Remember this, people will not go to much trouble to remember you and you'll never build a solid repeat and referral business by chance. You've got to cultivate it over time. The payoff is that the longer you are in the business and the more "old friends" you get to sell the fewer SOBs you'll have to deal with.

Let me relate two buying experiences my wife and I had recently. In one instance, a real estate agent sold us a vacation property on the beach that cost mega bucks. He spent only three hours with us and showed us four properties, and we bought one. We went from the property to his office to write up the offer, which was accepted, and the deal was done.

In the second instance, we had a very enjoyable dinner at a restaurant in a city where I was speaking at a convention. We were at the restaurant approximately two hours and spent less than $200.

One of these establishments sent us a gracious note after the sale. The other enterprise hasn't contacted us again since we finished our business with them. Care to guess who followed up: the real estate agent making the big buck transaction or the waiter making the $200 sale? You guessed it: While we never received so much as a thank-you note from the realtor who made the seven figure sale, we did get a unique thank-you postcard from Emeril Lagasse's Tchoup Chop Restaurant in Orlando, with a personal handwritten message signed by both our servers from that evening. BAM!

Would you care to calculate the amount of repeat and referral business the real estate agent is costing himself by failing to create a cult of loyal buyers? Do you have any inkling of what it's costing *you* if you're not? You never know whom you might influence with your follow-up efforts that separate you from the crowd. Nor do you know whom you might offend by your indifference.

I have never understood salespeople who treat following up with their customers like it was punishment. They never make a call or send a card or newsletter unless their manager nags them. If this is you, I recommend you go home tonight and apologize to your family for failing to provide for them at the level you could, and you should also beg their forgiveness for having to spend more time at work and less time with them because you've got to chase down new customers to compensate for those you've abused through neglect over the years. In a sense, salespeople who don't follow up with a customer after the sale are committing embezzlement from their company and their family.

C. Prospect for new business starting with the places you do business. Take responsibility for building your own pipeline of traffic rather than complaining that there isn't enough walking through the door. Too many salespeople sit back and whine because there aren't enough prospects to talk to and everyone they do get is an SOB. How many prospects have you gone out and found on your own? How many do you bring into your business on an average week? If you can't convincingly answer these two questions, it's time to stop blaming and get out there and break a sweat to build your own business within a business and create a cult of loyal customers. You're not a victim. And don't misinterpret what I mean by prospecting. I'm not talking about paging through the phone book making cold calls. What I am suggesting is that prospecting is just doing a more proactive job of letting people know who you are, what you do, and where you work by starting at the same places where you do business and spend your money. Once you do this, you will uncover new prospects for your product or service as a natural consequence.

You will never be consistently great in sales without building a pipeline of future business. You must master the paradox of making a sale today while at the same time you plant seeds for tomorrow. If you want a six-figure income in sales, you must discipline yourself to do both.

SOB Summary for Chapter 7: Create a Cult!

1. Set a goal to make yourself less dependent on fresh customers over time by building a strong repeat and referral business.

2. Don't join the club. Stay focused on the productive activities necessary to create your own cult.

3. Understand Girard's Law of 250. You cannot anger customers and expect to build your own business within a business. Good words about you get around fast, but negative words about you make the rounds even faster.

4. Treat your customers better than anyone else. Out think, out maneuver, and just plain outwork your competitors so that your customers would find it painful to have to deal with another salesperson.

5. Send mailers that actually get read. Sending mailers is a form of marketing, but there's a lot of competition for people's time today so you must be unique and make yours stand out. What you say in your mailer is less important than the fact that the customer saw your name in front of them yet again.

6. Build a pipeline of future customers. The only way you can expect to work with fewer SOBs in sales over time is to proactively build your own future by prospecting for new customers and not relying solely on what your company's advertising brings in or what leads your sales manager feeds you.

8 | Create Urgency to Buy Today!

Let's Start with Straight Talk

Many salespeople are afraid to build urgency for the customer to buy today because they're reluctant to appear as high pressure. Others go about trying to build urgency the wrong way and cause prospects to feel stressed and resist the salesperson by turning into an SOB. If you think you can sell the customer today you're probably right. And if you think you can't sell them today you're also right because it all starts with a state of mind. You're more likely to have the right state of mind if you possess the skills to back it up and the belief that the customer wants to get the purchase behind him. He is spread thin, and he doesn't have time to shop indefinitely for what you're selling, regardless of what he tells you. Stop making up reasons why the customer can't or won't buy sooner and start planting the seeds for him to make a faster purchase. Stop talking yourself out of more deals than you make by making it easy for the prospect to leave and go elsewhere or to "think it over." Stop letting your customer and yourself off the hook because you've never learned that the difference between pressure and persistence is technique. Let's get you ready to start selling with more urgency by embracing the strategies in the following pages.

Six Steps to Create Urgency to Buy Today!

1. You must believe that the customer will buy today. As stated in the opening paragraph of this chapter, if you think the customer will buy today, you're right. If you think the customer will find a reason to delay his or her purchase, you're right. Your own level of expectation shows up in your words, deeds, pace, and attitude toward the customer's purchase.

Three Fast Facts on Creating or Deflating Urgency to Buy Today:

A. Many salespeople talk people out of doing something *now*. Because droves of salespeople still walk around with a powerful fear of rejection, they take the pressure off themselves and the customer by saying or doing things that make it easy for the customer to procrastinate doing anything now and wait instead for a "better time." The good news is that the salesperson doesn't feel as strong a sense of rejection when he or she subtly pushes the prospect away from the immediate sale and the customer leaves without buying. The bad news is that the salesperson missed the sale and the prospect misses the product.

B. Prospects do more research today before they buy a product. This means they are more and not less ready to buy by the time they talk to you about your product. Since there is more information available to consumers today through the Internet and other sources, they are more educated and ready to buy than in past years. The information available to them is a reason to speed up, not delay the purchase process.

C. In spite of the facts presented in point B, prospects will still use the "I've just started looking" statement as a way to slow down salespeople. Don't buy into this. It is a natural defense mechanism. Remember that every time you're in front of a customer a sale is made. You either sell them on why it makes sense to move forward with the purchase *now,* or they sell you on the fact that they're still looking.

2. Take the fear out of buying now. One reason people want to delay a purchase is because they fear making a mistake. Knowing this in advance, use phrases and techniques that remove this fear.

Phrases to use at the appropriate time to remove the fear of buying now:

"Mr. Prospect, part of my job is to make this make sense for you. Is there any information you need clarified or additional information you require before we move forward?"

"Mr. Prospect, part of my job is to help you make the best decision possible and to stop you from making a mistake. Do you have any concerns that we should address now before moving forward?"

These questions help surface any concerns, objections, or future obstacles that could pop up and derail your efforts to close the deal later. By meeting them head-on, rather than hoping that they don't exist, you stay on track to make the sale now rather than let a concern fester and become a reason to delay a decision later.

3. Plant seeds of urgency to buy early and often. Don't wait until you're trying to close the deal to create urgency. By then, you can sound desperate and insincere. By planting seeds of urgency early in the sales process and by reinforcing them throughout the sales process you build credibility in the need to buy *now*.

4. Use "similar situation" stories to show how others benefited from acting *now*. Similar situation stories are powerful sales tools that create mental pictures that help you create both desire for gain and fear of loss.

5. Focus the prospect on the cost of doing nothing. To create urgency to buy now shift your customer's focus away from the cost of moving forward and toward the cost of doing nothing or the cost of procrastinating.

  A. Prices go up.

  B. Their trade-in value goes down.

  C. Rebates disappear.

  D. Interest rates rise.

  E. Interest rates may go down (if you're selling financial instruments).

  F. The product they want is no longer available.

  G. They fail to create momentum or drive traffic to their business.

  H. Lower morale as a result of point G.

I. They lose good employees as a result of point G.

J. The best days and time slots always go first.

K. They make themselves vulnerable to financial ruin (if you're selling insurance products).

Don't unload all of these points on top of customers as a last-ditch closing effort right before they're getting ready to leave. Sprinkle them (plant seeds) at appropriate points throughout the sales process and you'll slowly turn up the heat and make it make more sense to buy now.

6. Use the "that's exactly why you should do it now" close when prospects try to procrastinate. I listed this technique in Chapter 4, ut it is also appropriate to use in instances where you're creating more urgency as well. This script uses reverse psychology by taking a prospect's major objection and using it as a reason to move forward with the purchase now—even if it isn't exactly the deal he or she had hoped for. Read over this example used in car sales and see if you can apply a version of it to what you sell, be it homes, insurance, mortgages, or investments.

PROSPECT: The payment is just too high, the price is just too high, I'm not getting enough for my trade-in, etc.

SALESPERSON: Mr. Prospect, if the price seems too high now then that's exactly why you should take it. Since prices only go up over time, the value of trade-ins go down over time, and since interest rates are still on the rise, the longer you wait the worse things will get for you. I know this may not have been exactly what you had hoped to get when you came in, but it's a much better deal than you'll get if you wait and return later—especially after the rebate goes away or the car you're trading in has even more miles on it. Part of my job is to make this make sense for you and to stop you from making a mistake, so let's lock this deal in right now while you can guarantee the price on the product you want and maximize the value of your trade-in.

How to Persuade SOBs Who Don't Want to Be Persuaded to Buy Today

Persuading SOBs who don't want to be persuaded to buy today doesn't mean you must wrestle them to the ground and pin them until they cry, "I'll take it!" It means you apply techniques that create the proper conditions to buy now and let the customer's mind do the rest. Staying with our automotive sales example, examine these techniques and apply the principles to the products and services you sell.

Five Rules for Persuading SOBs Who Don't Want to be Persuaded:

1. Follow up your hot button determining question with a question designed to *narrowly define* what is most important to the prospect. Then zero in on that narrowly defined need and show how your product meets it.

> SALESPERSON: Mr. Prospect, what will be most important to you in your new car?
>
> PROSPECT: Something economical to maintain.
>
> SALESPERSON: How will you determine that the car you buy is meeting that need?
>
> PROSPECT: When I'm not "nickeled and dimed" by repairs and can start paying less than $200 per month for gas.

From this point on you can prove how the vehicle's warranty and fuel economy will eliminate "nickel and diming."

By narrowly focusing on and meeting the customer's self-spoken need, you remove potential objections and give reasons to buy now since what is admittedly most important to them is being addressed by your product or service.

2. Ask closing questions when you are in rapport with the prospect. The timing for when you ask a closing question is crucial. Being "in rapport" with the prospect means that you are in synch with him or her. This doesn't normally happen by accident but through deliberate technique. Let's take the rapport-building techniques used back in Chapter Three to an even higher level with the following points:

Four Tips for Getting "in Rapport" with a Prospect:

A. Don't invade the prospect's private space. This space is defined by sales psychologists as an 18-inch bubble around the entire body of the customer. At the same time, leaving the optimal space of between 19 inches and four feet from a prospect creates the risk of losing the focus or attention of the prospect. The ideal sales space between your nose and the prospect's is between 24–48 inches. Violate this space at your own risk.[1]

While I was shopping at an upscale men's store with my wife to look at a pair of shoes, a well-dressed salesperson with "Bob" on his name badge got right up in our faces and asked if I'd like to try on a pair of the shoes. This fellow soon had three strikes against him: (a) he invaded our private space; (b) he had breath that would knock a buzzard off a carcass; (c) his body odor indicated that the terror alert under his arms had been elevated to orange. The fact that he invaded our private space made the other two offenses noticeable much more quickly. Needless to say, B.O. Bob didn't sell me any shoes that day.

B. Pace your customer's speed, tone, and, to a large degree, his or her mood (unless it is downright ornery or negative). Since people tend to converse at a pace that is consistent with the speed of their thought process you risk losing them and falling out of rapport when your pace doesn't match their own. Here's a tip: It is both appropriate and desirable to pick up your pace a bit when transitioning into the product presentation in order to create an emotional boost of adrenaline. However, when closing the deal, it's important that your approach be casual, sincere, and matter-of-fact rather than too dramatic.[2]

C. Rally around a common cause and against a common enemy. Nothing binds two people, groups, or countries like a common cause or a common enemy. Find your customer's pet causes or enemies and align yourself with that viewpoint. Through your rapport-building questions and conversation you may discover that your prospect loves working with underprivileged kids, intramural softball, or environmental issues. You may also uncover that he hates high gas prices, loud and hokey commercials, gangs, drugs, the IRS, etc. As your conscience allows, get on the prospect's side of these issues and you will move closer to the sale and make a friend for life.[3]

D. Hang on their every word. Pay rapt attention to every word that comes out of your customer's mouth. Make it clear that what they have to say is the most important thing in either of your worlds at the moment because it is. When you show your customers this level of respect and attitude toward their life, business, and needs you shouldn't have to use an entire arsenal of closing tactics to make the sale, they'll insist you sell them and now![4]

Hanging on their every word is a significant tool for moving SOBs with an unhurried purchasing deadline into "fast forward" or those who may be indifferent or likely to shop around at a snail's pace more quickly toward the sale. They won't want to risk having to deal with a rude, apathetic, or unprofessional salesperson elsewhere.

3. Begin your presentation with a word, phrase, fact, or statistic that will blow them away. Don't just say, "*Consumer Reports* rates this car as #1 in its class." Do your homework and find out how many vehicles are in that specific class and make your statement bolder: "*Consumer Reports* rates this car as #1 out of 10 worldwide manufacturers and 22 different models." Rather than state your radio station is ranked #1 by Arbitron in a particular time slot, say that it is number #1 out of 6, 7, 8, etc. competitors. Go beyond saying that your financial institution has the highest interest-paying checking account in the state. How many financial institutions are in the state? Find out and say, "We have a higher interest-bearing checking account than the other 4,200 financial institutions in the state." These compelling and specific arguments for buying from you will create urgency and get even the most stubborn, obnoxious, or belligerent customer on your side quickly.

Do not exaggerate or make claims you cannot back up. But realize that by spending an hour or so with a good Internet search engine, you can come up with facts and figures about your market and your competitors that may have taken you days or weeks to track down just a few years ago. These stats will make you more persuasive and professional.

4. Use the "fear-not factor" to intrigue people and motivate them to move forward with the purchase. The key to this technique is moving people past the fear of making a decision. It is vital that you use a low-key, casual manner when saying the following scripts and not one that can come off as cocky or confrontational. It is quite effective in moving on-the-fence SOBs into a relationship with your company.

Examples of how to use the "fear-not factor" successfully:

"Mr. Prospect, one of your key decisions will be whether or not you're willing to leave your comfort zone and separate yourself from the pack with this purchase. If you feel up to the challenge, just say the word and I'll start the paperwork."

"Mr. Prospect, stepping up and reaching for something you've always dreamed of can be really exciting as well as a bit scary, but if you're ready to leave yesterday behind, just tell me how you'd like the title to read."

"Mr. Prospect, creating a message that is not only different but better takes guts. If you feel your company is ready to shake off the status quo and do what others are afraid to do, we'll go the second mile in putting the campaign together for you. The ball is in your court. Where do I go from here?"

Appropriately using the fear-not factor creates positive and challenging emotional conditions where people who might normally be happy with what they have or who would look for a reason to delay a purchase—because they're afraid to make a decision and move forward—enthusiastically step into new territory. In fact, doing so makes them feel energized, adventuresome, and more alive.

5. Argue against yourself. Every good speaker, politician, attorney and salesperson learns early on the value of taking the fight out of your opponent's argument by stealing their thunder and arguing against yourself. This psychology can quickly make you look more objective and open people up to what you have to say right before it closes the sale for you.[5]

Examples of Arguing Against Yourself:

"Mr. Prospect, if you want to try to save more money than we're offering right now, you could always wait to see if interest or insurance rates come back down. And if we're lucky, we'll still have the model you want."

"As long as you don't mind strangers coming to your door and driving your car, you might want to try and sell your trade-in yourself. Of course, I'd recommend that you call and verify their insurance and check for a valid license so you're not liable if they have an accident while driving your car."

"Mr. Prospect, you always have the option of doing nothing and hoping your business turns around and that something prompts more prospects to come through your doors. I've found there are two ways to get to the top of an oak tree: You can start climbing it or just sit on the acorn. Which do you believe is most practical for your business? (You can also use the "acorn" analogy when trying to convince buyers to invest in their future, with retirement accounts, college funds, or other financial instruments, or when selling memberships to fitness centers, weight loss programs, and the like.)

"Mr. and Ms. Prospect, even though we've had 26 rate increases in the past few years, you can always take your chances and hope that mortgage rates go back down again soon."

"Mr. Prospect, you can always just think positive and hope you're never injured or sick and that your kids all earn full scholarships to college."

When used with the right tone, at the right time, and under the right circumstances, this reverse psychology will close the sale like a steel trap. Think of potential scenarios and scripts in advance that you can use in the right situations.

SOB Summary for Chapter 8: Create Urgency to Buy Today!

1. You must believe the customer will buy today. Selling with urgency starts in the mind of a salesperson. If your expectations of the customer are too low, they tend to live down to them. Expect them to buy today and make it make sense for them to do so.

2. Take the fear out of buying today with carefully worded phrases like, "Part of my job is to stop you from making a mistake," "My job is to make this make sense to you," and so forth.

3. Use "similar situation" stories to show how others benefited from acting *now.* Use credible, real-life stories of how other people you know or sold benefited by acting with urgency. You can also relate examples of the penalties some people paid by not moving fast enough.

4. Focus your customer on the cost of doing nothing. The natural tendency is for a prospect to get immobilized by the cost of moving forward. You must help stop him from making a mistake by clearly pointing out the much more substantial penalty for doing nothing.

5. Use the "that's exactly why you should do it now" close. Apply reverse psychology by taking the primary objection a prospect gives you and then using it as a major reason why they should buy today.

6. Persuade people who don't want to be persuaded by narrowly defining their biggest want/need and showing how your product/service meets it, and remember that this removes potential objections later.

7. Only ask closing questions when you are in rapport with the prospect.

8. Begin your presentation with a word, phrase, fact, or statistic that will blow your customers away.

9. Use the fear-not factor to convert the fear they have of moving forward into a positive step in the right direction.

10. Use reverse psychology by arguing against yourself and making it even more obvious as to why your prospect should buy without you having to apply pressure.

9 | Learn to Read an SOB's Mind!

Let's Start with Straight Talk

Millions of salespeople make a good living selling their product in spite of the fact that they remain ignorant of how to read a customer's mind. How do you learn to read minds? It has nothing to do with psychics and everything to do with listening intently for what the customer *isn't* saying, learning all you can about human nature, and becoming a student of body language. The fact that so many salespeople make a good living while they remain ignorant of these skills is clear proof of what an incredibly high-potential profession selling remains. The thought that should keep salespeople up at night is, "If I'm doing this well without paying much attention to reading minds, how many more sales could I have made each month had I taken the time to upgrade my skills in this area?" And what should make everyone in sales bound out of bed each morning is the possibility of doubling or tripling their income if they'd start to learn to read minds now!

In order to read an SOB's mind you've got to discipline yourself to focus more on the customer and pay closer attention to his or her every move and non-move. By following the insightful strategies in this chapter you'll be on your way to creating faster, more profitable sales—even with the toughest customers.

1. Learn to listen between the lines. While you may be quite good at hanging on every word of the customer, you've got to take your listening skills a step further and pay closer attention to what isn't being said. What is not being said often reveals much more than what is. Learn to listen between the lines to uncover motives, fears, and a prospect's real agenda. Here are four examples that will help you get through the façade a prospect puts up and move closer to the sale.

A. If SOBs don't mention any other products or services they are shopping or looking at to compare with yours, they often are. Don't be afraid to ask your prospect, "What other products or services are you looking at to compare to what we have to offer." By uncovering this as early as possible, you have a chance to compare your product to the other in your presentation and prevent it from coming up later as an excuse or a reason to leave and "think it over."

B. If prospects never bring up having to confer with someone else before making a decision, they often do. Dig a little with this question, "Will there be anyone helping you make a decision or is this totally up to your own discretion?" Just as in the prior example, by flushing this out through your own efforts you can adjust your presentation to address this situation rather than have it tossed out by the prospect at the end of your presentation as a reason to leave.

C. If you're selling big-ticket items that are normally financed, and the customer never mentions financing or how they intend to pay for the product/service, ask, "Have you looked into financing options on your own or is that something you'd like us to help you with?" This question normally generates a wide array of information from a prospect ranging from a confession of "credit challenges" to the amount of a down payment to an intention to pay cash to a specific interest rate he thinks he has available.

D. If a prospect doesn't say anything derogatory about the product/service during your presentation but doesn't say anything specifically positive, it is an indication that you're presenting the wrong product/service to fit the prospect. Ask the prospect at this stage; "Is this product pretty much what you had in mind when you came here today or does it lack something that's vitally important to you?" Unless asked, many prospects are not inclined to squash your enthusiasm and interrupt your presentation by telling you that they don't like what you're showing them. Thus, they act interested for awhile, think of a reason to leave, ask for your card, and you never hear from them again.

2. Understand five common facts of human nature. A key to reading a prospect's mind is to understand certain, common elements of human nature that almost all human beings feel the same about. This awareness provides the intelligence necessary to connect with the prospect and have what you say resonate with his or her hopes, fears, wants, and needs. Here are five common facts of human nature that will help you get inside your prospect's head.[1]

A. Almost everyone is afraid to look bad. The exception to this would seem to be many of the teenagers you see in the mall. But then again, they're convinced they look great.

B. Almost everyone works to avoid pain and once in pain will do what it takes to get out of it. This is exactly why focusing SOBs on the cost of doing nothing—and remaining in their painful state—is such a powerful tool to overcome their hang-ups on the costs involved with moving forward.

C. When people get their mind set on something, they want it now! This fact works to your advantage since prospects are doing more research before they buy and are more prepared than ever before to make a decision and make it now regardless of what they tell you about "thinking it over" or yours being the first place they shopped. Most prospects today don't really need to "think it over" because they've already thought it over before they ever laid eyes on you!

Knowing this, the next time someone tells you that she has just started looking and has no intention of buying today, don't get defensive or cop an attitude. Instead, look her in the eye and say this:

"Mrs. Prospect, I agree with you. Like you, I never like to buy the first time I look at something or the first place that I shop, but when I see something I really like and know it will solve my problem and the price is right, I give some very serious consideration to making an exception. Now let me show you and your husband what our product can do for you."

In a nice way this tells the SOB that you understand her feelings but you are not necessarily *accepting* her excuse because there are always *exceptions* to her excuse.

D. People want to make decisions that will make them look good to others. "Making a decision" has a negative association to some people, but since you know that people do want to make decisions that will make them look good to others, put a positive spin on making a decision with the following tactic:

"Mr. Prospect, would you agree that every step forward or upward begins with a decision? Would you also agree that the best things you have in life right now are the result of making a decision rather than inaction? In fact, you could say that wherever you are in life at this point is the result of decisions you've made in the past isn't it? This being the case, would you be willing to make a difficult decision now that could immediately improve your future?"

E. Most people only have a moderate amount of self-esteem. This is why listening more intently to what prospects have to say and hanging on their every word elevates you in their eyes as a natural consequence of your placing them on a pedestal.

Knowing these five insights into human nature will help you structure your presentation in a way that moves prospects smoothly and quickly toward what you are selling them. Ignore these five facts and you'll continue to waste your time running in circles, believing every word an SOB tells you, and losing far more sales than you ever make.

3. Become a student of body language. While there are always exceptions to the following clues to human behavior, the symptoms offered give a clear insight to what someone is really thinking or doing. In fact, oftentimes these signs are screaming out at you in an attempt to tell you to slow down, speed up, ask a closing question, or move on to something else. The signs are always there. This is not the question. The only question is whether or not you're paying enough attention and are educated enough in reading body language to catch them and benefit as a result. What an SOB doesn't tell you with his words he's telling you with nearly every other body part he has visible.

A. The following are some potential signs of dishonesty[2]:

(1) Shifting or wandering eyes.

(2) Licking lips.

(3) Inappropriate familiarity, such as patting, other touching, and getting too close (invading personal space).

(4) Any activity that obscures the face, eyes, or mouth, such as putting a hand over one's mouth while talking, rubbing the nose, or rapid blinking of the eyes.

(5) An exaggerated version of the "sincere, furrowed-brow look."

(6) Change in tone.

(7) Any type of exaggeration.

(8) Rapid speech.

(9) A smile that comes and goes very rapidly is generally the sign of an insincere smile. Genuine smiles come very slowly and fade very slowly.

(10) Fake emotion. If SOBs bang the table in anger after they yell, they're faking it, so go ahead and call

their bluff. Most emotion comes through before we find a way to verbalize it, not after.

The signs of honesty are just the opposite of those listed above. Honest people are normally relaxed and calm; they usually meet your gaze. To glean even more value from this section, you might review this list and determine how many of these dishonest traits you're guilty of that astute prospects may pick up on. If you are prone to exaggeration and spewing hyped-up claims, while you're patting a prospect inappropriately on the back as you ramble on a mile a minute licking your lips like a camel eyeing an oasis, you've got serious issues to resolve.

B. The following are some potential signs of boredom[3]:

(1) Gazing into the distance.

(2) Glancing at watch or other objects. Speakers learn how to read a crowd like this early on and you'd be well advised to do the same.

(3) Sighing heavily.

(4) Yawning.

(5) Crossing and uncrossing legs and arms.

(6) Tapping feet.

(7) Pointing one's body away from the other person.

(8) Shifting weight.

If you notice your prospects doing many of these things very often, I am probably safe in assuming that you're not selling very much. If members of the opposite sex have done these things around you throughout your life, I'm probably safe in assuming that you're still single.

C. The following are some potential signs of anger/hostility[4]:

(1) Hands on hips.

(2) Frequent repetition of certain phrases.

(3) Tightly closed fists.

(4) Redness in face.

(5) Arms folded firmly in front of chest.

(6) Locked jaw.

(7) Stiff, rigid posture.

(8) Frozen expression or glare.

Kind of sounds like a famous college basketball coach doesn't it? If you're putting your customer into these states very often, *please* go back and reread this book. You missed some key points along the way.

D. These are some potential signs of indecision[5]:

(1) Shifting back and forth in one's chair.

(2) Looking back and forth between two fixed objects.

(3) Tilting the head from side to side.

(4) Opening and shutting hands or moving one hand, then the other.

(5) Opening and closing one's mouth without saying anything.

I highly recommend you spend some time reviewing the signs in these four categories and deciding up front how you should respond and alter your course when SOBs are sending you these powerful messages. For instance, if someone is showing signs of boredom, you should do less talking and ask more questions, especially those that will help you determine if you're on the right track. If someone is showing signs of anger, you should probably go lower and slower with your speech and be certain you're not sending out body language that will escalate the situation.

4. Ask questions they're not expecting. To determine what people are thinking it's important to put them in situations for which they haven't mentally prepared themselves or rehearsed. In these cases their reaction will be more honest and help you read what is on their mind.

Samples of unexpected questions that offer clues for closing a client:

A. If you bought this RV today, who is the first person you'd show? Where is the first place you'd take it? In addition to creating mental ownership, the answer can reveal buying motives: pride/showing off, a practical purpose or upcoming need, etc.

B. What has held you back from advertising with our station/doing business with our bank/evaluating our investment products in the past? Don't be afraid to ask this question. It can reveal deep-seated fears, concerns, or problems that could cause SOBs to persist in their non-patronizing ways unless you uncover and address these issues.

Think of other unexpected questions you can ask during the rapport-building stage, the presentation, and when dealing with objections and closing the sale. Your objective is to ask questions that will reveal hidden thoughts, buying motives, reservations, or agendas.

To paraphrase C. S. Lewis, if you have rats in the cellar, you're more likely to see them if you go down quickly, before they have a chance to hide. The suddenness of your approach doesn't create the rats. It merely reveals those already there[6].

The same is true when you ask an unexpected or provocative question during a presentation or closing situation. The suddenness of your inquiry doesn't create an ill-tempered, sarcastic, or dishonest SOB; it merely reveals the ill-tempered, sarcastic, or dishonest SOB already there in front of you.

5. Pay more attention to *how* they say something than to what they say. Tone, inflection, pace, and the rhythm of someone's speech can tell you much more about what they're thinking than the words themselves. If someone has ever insincerely told you they were sorry, you know what I'm talking about. The words were right, but the tone may have betrayed anger, sarcasm, or insincerity. You simply must listen more closely to how something is being said: with sincerity, sarcasm, reservation, or conviction. If someone is displaying an emotion counterproductive to your making the sale, don't pretend it isn't happening. Deal with it. For instance, when an SOB says, "I don't *have* to buy anything today." You can respond with something like:

"John, it sounds like even though you may have a flexible timetable for making a purchase, if the right deal presented itself you could justify moving forward soon. Is this the case?"

I truly hope you fully appreciate what an edge the strategies in this chapter offer you over amateur salespeople who talk too much, listen too little, and never learn to read their customers' minds. Use this edge to help the customer make the right decision and to make yourself a much better living.

SOB Summary for Chapter 9: Learn to Read an SOB's Mind!

1. Listen to what isn't being said. The "iceberg" principle tells you that the part of the iceberg you can see (or, in this case, the words the customer is actually saying) is a small part of the actual structure. The part that can sink the ship (or cost you the sale) lies under the surface and is not visible.

2. Learn the five common facts of human nature: (a) Almost everyone is afraid to look bad; (b) almost everyone works to avoid pain and, once in pain, will do what it takes to get out; (c) when people set their mind on something, they want it now!; (d) people want to make decisions that will make them look good to others; (e) most people have only a moderate amount of self-esteem.

3. Become a student of body language so you can pick up signs of dishonesty, boredom, anger/hostility, or indecision.

4. Ask questions the SOBs are not expecting in order to get a less rehearsed and more honest answer.

5. Pay more attention to *how* something is said rather than simply what is being said. Does their tone betray sarcasm, dishonesty, insincerity, or excitement?

10

Be Prepared to Walk Away!

Let's Start with Straight Talk

As paradoxical as it sounds, you'll make more deals if you aren't so worried about losing them. Yes, more often than not, the more you want a deal, the less likely you are to get it. The bottom line is this: When you're mentally and physically prepared to walk away from a sale you'll find that you don't have to very often. Because salespeople haven't disciplined their emotions to embrace this concept, SOBs push them around during the sales process far more often than they should. And if the salesperson does make the sale, it's normally for a minimal commission because the difficult customer wrung every last dime of profit out of the deal before the beleaguered salesman screamed "Uncle!" While you never want to lose a deal, it's important to realize that some sales and customers bring a negative value to you and your organization. The time invested in them isn't worth the profit—or lack of profit—that results. The passion and energy lost in brawling with a prospect leaves little left over to invest in normal prospects who recognize value and are willing to pay for it. The good news is that if you'll follow the guidelines in this book prospects are less likely to become ugly, and, even if they do, you'll be able to turn things around and sell profitably. In the following paragraphs I'll present two "lucky sevens": seven additional power phrases and closing techniques that you can add to the dozens of others in this book to make the sale. And in the event you lose the sale regardless of your best efforts, I'll present seven actions you can take to salvage it.

It's Not a Matter of Life and Death

If you look at every deal you have as "life or death," you'll be dead a lot. Do all you can to sell the customer but remember that sales is still a numbers game. Continue doing the right thing and the numbers will work out in your favor—even if you lose this one. Keep in mind that you can't make a good deal with a bad person. Some customers can never be satisfied. Don't get hung up on these few. Focus on the following techniques that will earn the customers worthy of your time and services.

Seven Power Phrases and Closes for the Most Difficult Customers

Use the following scripts when you're at the end of your rope and there is nothing else to lose when trying to close the deal or please a customer. Say these words sincerely and courteously when the situation warrants:

1. **The "expert negotiator" close.**

    "Mr. Customer, I'd like to accommodate your demands—truly I would. But from a business standpoint there's a difference between giving a great deal and letting yourself be taken advantage of by an expert negotiator. Frankly, we can't stay in business to service our customers if we let that happen very often, so if you agree that while maybe this isn't everything you wanted but is still more than fair, let's shake hands and make the deal." (Then zip your lips and extend your hand.)

2. The "greater concern" close.

"Mr. Prospect, I understand that one of your concerns in buying this new car is money. But I'm sure an even greater concern is making a choice that will best serve your family for the next several years. What poses a greater risk for you: paying a bit more than you originally expected or not getting the vehicle your family wants, needs, and deserves?"

"Mr. Prospect, I understand that one of your concerns in buying this insurance protection is affordability. But I'm sure an even greater concern is making a choice that will best protect your family's future in the result of your untimely death. What poses a greater risk for you: paying a bit more than you originally expected or not protecting your family with what it is going to need to survive and thrive in your absence?"

3. The "it's not my best price" close.

Here's the situation: You've grinded out a deal with a tough customer and then he or she puts you on the spot by asking, "Is this absolutely your best price? Sharpen your pencil because I know you can do better than that!"

Don't get defensive; instead, lower your tone just a bit and speak slowly and sincerely when you reply with: "No, Mr. Prospect, it is not my very best price." (At this point the customer's eyes will bulge and his or her mouth may drop open.) "I can probably give you a lower price than what I just quoted, but it will have to come out of my pocket, and I can't work for nothing any more than you can. I'm sure you wouldn't want that for me anymore than I'd want that for you. However, since this is a very fair price, is there anything else that would stop us from moving forward today?"[1]

4. The "I'll be right back" close.

Here's the situation: Customers are sitting in your office after you've made a presentation and asked a closing question, and they reply with, "We'll need to think this over."

Smile, stand up, and say, "Fine, I'm going to go out back and get myself a cup of coffee. I'll be back in 15 to 20 minutes so you folks can talk it over. Can I bring you something back?"[2]

5. The "empathy not sympathy" close.

The customer gives you the longest sob story you've ever heard about why she or he can't afford your product or service. It might sound something like this:

PROSPECT: "There's no way we can afford that extra $50 per month. We just bought braces for the twins and have had to help mother pay her hospital bills. Sally had her hours cut at work and we're getting deeper in debt. In fact, we've run up $30,000 in credit card debt over the past two years alone."

SALESPERSON: "Mr. Prospect, other than the things you've just told me, is there anything else holding you back from moving forward with the purchase today?"

PROSPECT: a little taken aback with disbelief: "No, but I think what I told you ought to be enough reason!"

SALESPERSON: "Mr. Prospect, frankly, there are vehicles I can sell you for $50 less per month if the money is what's most important to you. But, based on what you told me when you came in, it won't be the vehicle that will meet the needs for you, your wife, and the twins. Think about it this way, if you're already $30,000 in debt, an extra $50 per month over what you expected to pay won't make much difference, and for that $1.75 per day more than you had hoped to pay, you'll get what you really want and need and won't have to settle for less. In the midst of all your other troubles, this new vehicle could become the one truly bright spot that turns your luck around."

Remember, in selling it is important to be empathetic but not sympathetic. The difference between empathy and sympathy is the loss of objectivity. Don't lose sight of the fact that your objective is to get the prospect involved with your product or service and to sell it to him or her as quickly as possible.

6. The "just say no to nibbles" close.

Situation: You've nearly consummated the deal, but the prospect tries to get one last concession from you (a nibble). It might sound something like this:

PROSPECT: "Tell your boss that if he throws in the extended warranty I'll take it today."

At this point, if you go and check with your boss you've committed a major negotiation flaw: You will have given the customer hope! If you have good rapport with the prospect, you should be able to brush most of the nibbles that you ever hear away with a phrase like this:

SALESPERSON: "I don't blame you for trying, Mr. Prospect. But you've worked us over so thoroughly on the price, I couldn't throw in a slice of cheese for a Whopper. Just sign here and we'll have you home in time for dinner."

At this point, the prospect will probably say, "Well, I had to try." Of course he did. You can't blame the SOB for trying. He just wants to make sure he's getting the best deal possible. By offhandedly brushing these nibbles aside—without having to go check with your manager—you'll maintain high profit levels and happier customers. After all, the last thing you want the customer to believe is that she didn't get the best deal she could have. If you pop up like a jack-in-the-box to go check with your manager and then come back with a concession, you've just opened the door to the possibility that she is still not getting the best deal, and she's likely to continue pushing you around until you've sold the product at a commission equal to minimum wage.

Stay with the Customer!

In addition to "just say no to nibbles," I've provided other techniques throughout the book that will arm you to stay with an SOB and negotiate before having to check with your manager or get approval from some higher authority. The "maintenance close" and "reduce it to the ridiculous" strategy for justifying a higher payment as presented in Chapter 3 are tools you can use in this regard, as is the "if it's too high then that's exactly why you should take it" technique outlined in Chapter 8. The longer you can stay with your prospect without having to go check with your boss, three things will happen: (a) Your price will have more credibility, (b) you'll close the deal more quickly, and (c) you'll close the deal at a higher profit.

7. The "for reasons of my integrity" close.

In Chapter 1, I mentioned Eric Samuelson, who does an incredible job running the preemployment profiling, hiring, and coaching division of LearnToLead. Eric deals with business owners all over the world who buy our assessment products, and he related the following strategy to me that you may be able to use depending on what you sell.

"A tough customer that had inquired about our preemployment assessments but never purchased called back after five months of my leaving unanswered messages to follow up our initial conversation. He said that he really liked our system and his only holdback was the price. He 'wondered if there was anything new.' Of course I took that to mean he wanted to know if there was anything new with the pricing. I replied, 'There's a lot new. We have added several dozen clients since we spoke last.' I told him how record sales months were being recorded at many of our clients' businesses and that the leaders there were reporting that bad hires were being virtually eliminated.

"He asked if I could 'help him out on the price.' I replied, 'For reasons of my integrity, everyone buys off the same price chart. That applies to Mr. Smith with his 11 outlets and Mr. Jones on the Louisiana bayou who has a total of 12 employees.'

"I built some more value, citing the addition of the Group Profiles feature, the upcoming Interview System, and the Anderson Sales Test, which we are beta testing. I told him I'd be willing to help him out understanding the profiles and that we intended this to be a relationship, not merely a transaction. I said, 'We are hoping that you see us as highly reliable partners in helping you make wise hiring decisions.'

"He said, 'Let's do it.'

"I said, 'What size pack do you want?'

"So, he did what any sensible business owner would do and placed a $12,000 order!"

Seven Things to Do When You Lose a Sale

Sometimes, despite your most diligent efforts and highly developed skills, you lose the deal. It may be when the customer says "no." Other times it is when a customer backs out after the contract is already signed. While you cannot choose what happened to cause the lost sale, you can choose your response. By following the seven steps for what to do when you lose a sale, you can still make the time you have invested in the SOB pay big dividends.

1. Save the sale! Don't give up too soon. Dig, dig, and persist until you either make the deal or honestly determine the deal is dead. Sales expert and author Ralph Roberts estimates that 75% of "lost deals" can be saved if the salesperson will stay positive, persistent, and creative.[3] I know a car salesman in New Hampshire who persistently follows up until the prospect either buys or dies and, when he hears that a prospect has died, it is rumored that he attends the wake just to be sure!

2. Find out why. The feedback you receive can help you improve and make the lost sale pay you back many times in the future. Ask the customer, "I'm always trying to improve my skills, so please tell me why you decided to wait/buy from another. You won't hurt my feelings. You'll help me get better." Then learn from the response.[4]

3. Stay in contact with the customer. You may have lost a battle, but you can still win the war. Many times customers regret their decision to go elsewhere almost immediately after their purchase. Keep your foot in the door. Keep them on your mailing list and call and ask, "How are they treating you? Is everything OK?" I can assure you that these SOBs will send you referrals and come in to buy from you the next time they're in the market for what you sell.[5]

4. Thank them for their time. Send thank-you cards thanking them for their time and consideration. This one act differentiates you from 99% of salespeople. Not only will this set you up for future referrals and purchases from this client, it will make an even higher-impact impression if the person who made the sale hasn't followed up.[6]

5. Ask for a referral. If you follow the above steps, referrals will be even easier for you to gain from a sale you lost. Don't be afraid to ask for referrals. Many times the reason prospects bought elsewhere will not inhibit them from sending you their friends. By asking, you also keep the door open for a future relationship with the lost-sale customer.[7]

6. Move on! If you view a lost sale as a learning opportunity you will be ready to move on and make the next sale, which is probably right around the corner. Don't take the loss personally. It's part of the business. Believe in the laws of numbers and know that this lost sale just moved you closer to your next deal.[8]

7. Make a graceful exit.

Here's the situation: The customer just turned down your best deal and is ready to leave. Nothing you've tried has worked, and you have no more room to negotiate on price.

Leave the customers with a very favorable impression of you and your business. Stay professional, upbeat, and mature. Say something like:

"Mr. and Mrs. Prospect, I'm very sorry things didn't work out for us today. But I do want to say how nice it was to meet you and have the opportunity to earn your business. If you do reconsider and decide you'd like to do business, please let me know right away. You'll never regret owning our product or choosing me as your salesperson."

When you miss a sale it is even more important to make a cheerful, friendly, optimistic, and courteous exit than it is when you make a sale. This is because the prospect is going to immediately start justifying his or her decision—whether it was a yes or no. If the answer is yes, the prospect will talk primarily about the product and secondarily about the salesperson. But if the answer is no and there has been any personality conflict, you can be sure that the negative comments will be about the salesperson.[9]

Two Parting Thoughts

As our journey to sell more, to sell more quickly, to sell at higher profits, and to do all of this while selling to SOBs comes to an end, I want to leave you with two final thoughts.

1. There is no way you got all you can out of this book by reading it only once. This book is designed to be studied and not skimmed through or read for amusement. Go through it again and again. Take the techniques most applicable to what you do and turn them into weekly training themes for your own personal growth. Referring regularly to your highlighted passages and the SOB summaries found at the conclusion of each chapter will keep you sharp.

2. Stay stupid. In other words, regardless of how successful you become or how much money you make, don't turn into a know-it-all. Stay stupid, remain teachable and open minded, listen to others, and continue to learn all you can about human nature and the art of selling. The key to becoming great in sales is to never believe you're great—even if you are.

"Even if you're on the right track, you'll get run over if you just sit there." —Will Rogers

---

SOB Summary for Chapter 10: Be Prepared to Walk Away!

1. You'll make more sales if you're not so worried about losing them. The more prepared you are to walk away from a deal, the less you'll have to.

2. Use the seven power phrases and closes to sell the SOB today:

   A. The "expert negotiator" close.

   B. The "greater concern" close.

   C. The "it's not my best price" close.

   D. The "I'll be right back" close.

   E. The "empathy not sympathy" close.

   F. The "just say no to nibbles" close.

   G. The "for reasons of my integrity" close.

3. When you lose a deal there are seven things to do:

   A. Save the deal!

   B. Find out why!

   C. Stay in contact with the customer.

   D. Thank them for their time.

   E. Ask for referrals.

   F. Move on!

   G. Make a graceful exit.

Notes

Chapter 3

1. Jeffrey Gitomer, *The sales bible* (Hoboken, NJ: Wiley, 2003), 207.

Chapter 6

1. Roger Dow & Susan Cook, *Turned on* (New York: HarperCollins, 1996), 15.
2. Ibid., 30.
3. Ibid., 156.
4. Zig Ziglar, *Ziglar on selling* (Nashville, TN: Thomas Nelson, 2003), 231–232.

Chapter 7

1. Joe Girard, *How to sell anything to anybody* (New York: Warner Books, 1977), 11–12.
2. Ibid., 62–63.
3. Ibid., 66.
4. Ibid., 58.
5. Ibid., 94.
6. Ibid., 78–79.

Chapter 8

1. Kevin Hogan, *The science of influence* (Hoboken, NJ: Wiley, 2005), 26–27.
2. Ibid., 40.
3. Ibid., 43.
4. Ibid., 45.
5. Ibid., 65.

Chapter 9

1. Ibid., 172–173.
2. Jo-Ellan Dimitrius, Ph.D, *Reading people* (New York: Random House, 1998), 59–60.
3. Ibid., 62.
4. Ibid., 63.
5. Ibid., 67–68.
6. C. S. Lewis, *Mere Christianity* (New York: HarperCollins, 1952), 192.

Chapter 10

1. Ziglar, *Ziglar on Selling,* 211.
2. Ibid., 210.
3. Ralph Roberts, *52 weeks of sales success* (New York: HarperCollins, 1999), 96.
4. Ibid., 97.
5. Ibid., 98.
6. Ibid., 99.
7. Ibid., 99.
8. Ibid., 99.
9. Ziglar, *Ziglar on selling,* 150.

Bibliography

Anderson, D. (1999). *Selling above the crowd*. Nashville, TN: Horizon.

Bauer, J. & Levey, M. (2004). *How to persuade people who don't want to be persuaded*. Hoboken, NJ: Wiley.

Dimitrius, J. (1998). *Reading people*. New York: Random House.

Dow, R. & Cook, S. (1996). *Turned on*. New York: HarperCollins.

Girard, J. (1977). *How to sell anything to anybody*. New York: Warner Books.

Gitomer, J. (2003). *The sales bible*. Hoboken, NJ: Wiley.

Gitomer, J. (2005). *The little red book of selling*. Austin, TX: Bard Press.

Hogan, K. (2005). *The science of influence*. Hoboken, NJ: Wiley.

Lewis, C. S. (1952). *Mere Christianity*. New York: HarperCollins.

Roberts, R. (1999). *52 weeks of sales success*. New York: HarperCollins.

Ziglar, Z. (2003). *Ziglar on selling*. Nashville, TN: Nelson Business.